T0123482

An Analysis of

Eve Kosofsky Sedgwick's

Epistemology of the Closet

Christien Garcia

Published by Macat International Ltd
24:13 Coda Centre, 189 Munster Road, London SW6 6AW.

Distributed exclusively by Routledge
2 Park Square, Milton Park, Abingdon, Oxon OX14 4RN
711 Third Avenue, New York, NY 10017, USA

Routledge is an imprint of the Taylor & Francis Group, an informa business

www.macat.com
info@macat.com

Cataloguing in Publication Data
A catalogue record for this book is available from the British Library.
Library of Congress Cataloguing-in-Publication Data is available upon request.
Cover illustration: Etienne Gilfillan

ISBN 978-1-912453-57-3 (hardback)
ISBN 978-1-912453-12-2 (paperback)
ISBN 978-1-912453-27-6 (e-book)

Notice
The information in this book is designed to orientate readers of the work under analysis,
to elucidate and contextualise its key ideas and themes, and to aid in the development
of critical thinking skills. It is not meant to be used, nor should it be used, as a
substitute for original thinking or in place of original writing or research. References and
notes are provided for informational purposes and their presence does not constitute
endorsement of the information or opinions therein. This book is presented solely for
educational purposes. It is sold on the understanding that the publisher is not engaged
to provide any scholarly advice. The publisher has made every effort to ensure that
this book is accurate and up-to-date, but makes no warranties or representations with
regard to the completeness or reliability of the information it contains. The information
and the opinions provided herein are not guaranteed or warranted to produce particular
results and may not be suitable for students of every ability. The publisher shall not be
liable for any loss, damage or disruption arising from any errors or omissions, or from
the use of this book, including, but not limited to, special, incidental, consequential or
other damages caused, or alleged to have been caused, directly or indirectly, by the
information contained within.

CONTENTS

THE MACAT LIBRARY

The Macat Library is a series of unique academic explorations of seminal works in the humanities and social sciences – books and papers that have had a significant and widely recognised impact on their disciplines. It has been created to serve as much more than just a summary of what lies between the covers of a great book. It illuminates and explores the influences on, ideas of, and impact of that book. Our goal is to offer a learning resource that encourages critical thinking and fosters a better, deeper understanding of important ideas.

Each publication is divided into three Sections: Influences, Ideas, and Impact. Each Section has four Modules. These explore every important facet of the work, and the responses to it.

This Section-Module structure makes a Macat Library book easy to use, but it has another important feature. Because each Macat book is written to the same format, it is possible (and encouraged!) to cross-reference multiple Macat books along the same lines of inquiry or research. This allows the reader to open up interesting interdisciplinary pathways.

To further aid your reading, lists of glossary terms and people mentioned are included at the end of this book (these are indicated by an asterisk [*] throughout) – as well as a list of works cited.

Macat has worked with the University of Cambridge to identify the elements of critical thinking and understand the ways in which six different skills combine to enable effective thinking.
Three allow us to fully understand a problem; three more give us the tools to solve it. Together, these six skills make up the **PACIER** model of critical thinking. They are:

ANALYSIS – understanding how an argument is built
EVALUATION – exploring the strengths and weaknesses of an argument
INTERPRETATION – understanding issues of meaning

CREATIVE THINKING – coming up with new ideas and fresh connections
PROBLEM-SOLVING – producing strong solutions
REASONING – creating strong arguments

To find out more, visit **WWW.MACAT.COM.**

CRITICAL THINKING AND *EPISTEMOLOGY OF THE CLOSET*

Primary critical thinking skill: CREATIVE THINKING
Secondary critical thinking skill: INTERPRETATION

The deconstructive and poststructuralist methods Sedgwick uses in her examination of the homo/heterosexual definition are closely tied to the critical skills of creative thinking and interpretation. Deconstruction is a postmodern mode of analysis that seeks to undo binaries and hierarchies of meaning in order to reveal the underlying assumptions of a text or belief. Similarly, poststructuralism seeks—in a necessarily paradoxical way—to dismantle the sign systems that make meaning possible, thus offering new ways of thinking. Sedgwick uses deconstructive and poststructuralist techniques to complicate and build upon the work of Michel Foucault, whose work on relations of power, discourse, and sexuality is itself exemplary of postmodern practices of creative thinking and interpretation. Specifically, Sedgwick expands, and in a sense inverts, Foucault's famous thesis that homosexuality is an "invention" of modern disciplinary power. In *Epistemology of the Closet*, she shows how it is, in fact, the conceptual distinction between gay and straight—as unstable as it is—that produces the patterns and relations of modern thought— i.e., that homosexual definition is the basis, rather than merely the product, of disciplinary meaning. This playing with the sequentiality of homosexual definition and modern thought ("what came first, the chicken or the egg?") is a good example of Sedgwick's formidable skill in postmodern modes of critical thinking and interpretation.

ABOUT THE AUTHOR OF THE ORIGINAL WORK

Eve Kosofsky Sedgwick (1950-2009) was an American scholar, poet, and artist. Sedgwick is known for applying her training in literary criticism to investigate questions of desire, intimacy, and power, and she is perhaps most famous for her foundational contributions to the field of Queer Theory. Her textured analyses of literary texts and social relations have earned her a prominent place in the arenas of cultural studies, critical theory, and gender and sexuality studies. Her books include *Between Men: English Literature and Male Homosocial Desire* (1985), *Epistemology of the Closet* (1990), *Tendencies* (1993), *A Dialogue on Love* (1999), and *Touching Feeling: Affect, Pedagogy and Performativity* (2003). Today Sedgwick is remembered not only for her intellectual output, but also for her generosity and wit as a teacher, colleague, and creative interlocutor.

ABOUT THE AUTHOR OF THE ANALYSIS

Christien Garcia is a scholar of Visual Culture, and Gender and Sexuality Studies. He recently completed his PhD in English and Cultural Studies at McMaster University and is currently a Social Sciences and Humanities Research Council Postdoctoral Fellow.

ABOUT MACAT

GREAT WORKS FOR CRITICAL THINKING

Macat is focused on making the ideas of the world's great thinkers accessible and comprehensible to everybody, everywhere, in ways that promote the development of enhanced critical thinking skills.

It works with leading academics from the world's top universities to produce new analyses that focus on the ideas and the impact of the most influential works ever written across a wide variety of academic disciplines. Each of the works that sit at the heart of its growing library is an enduring example of great thinking. But by setting them in context – and looking at the influences that shaped their authors, as well as the responses they provoked – Macat encourages readers to look at these classics and game-changers with fresh eyes. Readers learn to think, engage and challenge their ideas, rather than simply accepting them.

'Macat offers an amazing first-of-its-kind tool for interdisciplinary learning and research. Its focus on works that transformed their disciplines and its rigorous approach, drawing on the world's leading experts and educational institutions, opens up a world-class education to anyone.'

Andreas Schleicher
Director for Education and Skills, Organisation for Economic Co-operation and Development

'Macat is taking on some of the major challenges in university education … They have drawn together a strong team of active academics who are producing teaching materials that are novel in the breadth of their approach.'

Prof Lord Broers,
former Vice-Chancellor of the University of Cambridge

'The Macat vision is exceptionally exciting. It focuses upon new modes of learning which analyse and explain seminal texts which have profoundly influenced world thinking and so social and economic development. It promotes the kind of critical thinking which is essential for any society and economy. This is the learning of the future.'

Rt Hon Charles Clarke, former UK Secretary of State for Education

'The Macat analyses provide immediate access to the critical conversation surrounding the books that have shaped their respective discipline, which will make them an invaluable resource to all of those, students and teachers, working in the field.'

Professor William Tronzo, University of California at San Diego

WAYS IN TO THE TEXT

KEY POINTS

- Sedgwick was an American academic, writer, artist, and activist best known for her foundational role in the development of Queer Theory.*

- Sedgwick shows how the oppositional definition of hetero/homosexuality structures (and damages) thinking itself.

- *Epistemology of the Closet* has the capacity to profoundly alter our understanding of the relationship between homosexuality and modern culture.

Who was Eve Kosofsky Sedgwick?

Born in 1950, Eve Kosofsky grew up in a middle-class family in Ohio and Maryland. Her mother was a schoolteacher and her father worked as a cartographer for NASA. She studied first at Cornell University and in 1975 received her doctorate from Yale University. As a scholar, Sedgwick brought traditional literary scholarship together with poststructuralism* in order to intervene in and build upon the emerging feminist and gay studies of the eighties. In this way, Sedgwick's work helped to lay the foundations of what is today known as Queer Theory, an analytic framework that blends various methodologies including psychoanalysis,* semiotics,* literary analysis, and grassroots activism in order to think through the complexities of sexuality, gender, and intimacy.

Sedgwick's methodological approach holds that the study of literature must happen alongside an interrogation of the broader society in which it is situated. Sedgwick's scholarship bears the imprint of her life-long involvement in political activism, particularly her involvement in community-led AIDS and anti-homophobia protest and organizing of the 1980s. In the 2008 preface to that edition of the book, Sedgwick emphasizes the influence that the 1980's AIDS crisis had on her work. "The need for mobilizing powerful resources of resistance in the face of such horror," she writes, "imprinted a characteristic stamp on much of the theory and activism of that time."[1] Sedgwick also reminds readers that the book was written in the wake of the "openly anti-gay" 1986 American Supreme Court decision *Bowers v. Hardwick*, in which the Court upheld a Georgian sodomy law. In the context of what Sedgwick saw as a deep-seated climate of cultural and instructional homophobia, *Epistemology of the Closet* offers a radical rethinking of the relationship between sexuality and broader society.

What does *Epistemology of the Closet* say?

How much of what we know about the world depends on the distinction between gay and straight sexuality? For Sedgwick, the answer is surprising. She argues that many of the categories we use to understand the world comes out of the seemingly unrelated conceptual distinction between homosexuality and heterosexuality. What's more, Sedgwick argues that this knowledge of the world—because it comes out of a reliance on the faulty oppositional dynamic of what she calls the hetero/homosexual definition (gay verses straight)—is fundamentally "damaged in its central substance."[2] If there is a one-sentence summary of the critical argument of *Epistemology of the Closet* it is that our understanding of Western culture is incomplete to the extent that it does not incorporate a critical analysis of the modern definitional distinction of gay/straight.

To break this down, we can look at three aspects of Sedgwick's argument: the pervasiveness of homo/heterosexuality as the basis of modern thought; the significance of the closet as the trope of experience; and the seemingly contradictory need to conceptualize same-sex desire outside the axis of sex (i.e., gender-based attraction). First, Sedgwick argues that the homo/heterosexual definition is not simply a product of Western ideas about identity and social organization; rather, it is the very basis of those formations. In other words, homosexuality might seem to be a particular issue affecting only a sub-section of the population, but things are not so simple. For Sedgwick, homosexuality runs to the very core of how all relations—be they between men and women, between the people and the state, or between ideas themselves—are constructed and negotiated in modern culture.

Second, *Epistemology of the Closet* problematized the notion of the closet, arguing that the complex relations of the known and the unknown, the explicit and the inexplicit that underpin it have the potential for being peculiarly revealing as a critical framework. In particular, Sedgwick reads and complicates these "closet relations" through the concept of performativity,* noting that "closetedness" is far from a straight-forward act of secrecy. It involves not simply staying silent but performing or "speaking" a kind of silence that accrues by virtue of the discourse* that surrounds and constitutes it.[3] In other words, the closet can be read as a kind of performance in that it interpolates people into the being of invisibility.

Finally, *Epistemology of the Closet* proposes an important intervention in the disciplinary frameworks of gay studies and feminist thought. Sedgwick argues that "it is unrealistic to expect a close, textured analysis of same-sex relations through an optic calibrated … to the coarser stigmata of gender difference."[4] Thus, Sedgwick posits a study of homosexuality along the axis of sexuality instead of the axis of gender. In doing so, charts exciting new directions for lesbian and gay studies, and feminism* alike. The aim here is a richer and more textured analytic method that can take into account the many dimensions of sexuality other than that of gender attraction. What's more, Sedgwick argues, you can't understand relations between men and women unless you understand the relationship between people of the same gender, including the possibility of a sexual relationship between them.

Why does *Epistemology of the Closet* matter?

At a time of increasingly liberalized attitudes towards homosexuality and of expanding gay rights such as marriage equality, it might seem that Sedgwick's work on the gay closet would be less relevant than it was in 1990 when *Epistemology of the Closet* was first published. It might well be argued, however, that the opposite is true. This is because much of the discourse around gay rights and marriage equality today perpetuates an essentialist framework of thinking about sexuality or what Sedgwick opposed. Above all, Sedgwick was invested in challenging what she called the "re-naturalizing of identity categories."[5] What does Sedgwick mean by this and why does it concern her? In order to reflect on this further we might take up the example of the contemporary gay mantra "born this way" popularized in part by the pop music singer Lady Gaga.* Sedgwick's argument in *Epistemology of the Closet* invites readers to question the baseline assumption of this expression—the suggestion that some people are simply born gay. Gayness or queerness* is, for Sedgwick, far more complex, diffuse, and pervasive than simply an innate quality that some people are affected by and others not. The view that homosexuality is something innate in only certain people is dangerous for Sedgwick because it obscures the ways in which sexuality is constructed relationally. The idea of homosexuality is only comprehensible in relation to the idea of heterosexuality, and thus the two are born of one another. Furthermore, the view that gay people are normal because they are born gay may be beneficial for advancing the acceptance of legal recognition of gays and lesbians, but it does so in a way that reproduces the discourse of what is and isn't "natural." And this gets to the heart of the problematic nature of what Sedgwick calls the "minoritizing view" of homosexuality.[6] In reply to "born this way," Sedgwick seems to ask, why do you have to be *born* this way in order to be permitted to *act* this way? Meanwhile, the complimentary maxim that gay people are "just like everyone else" or "human like everyone else" has, for Sedgwick, its own problems. In contrast to the minoritizing logic, the belief that gay people are the same as everyone else, only gay—or what Sedgwick calls the "universalizing view" of homosexuality—risks obscuring the complexity of sexual experience.[7] People *are* different from each other, and "it is astonishing," Sedgwick writes, "how few conceptual tools we have for dealing with this self-evident fact."[8] Thus, complicating and expanding the way we think about sexual difference, and the way the overly simplistic distinction between gay/straight over-determines modern culture, is the central preoccupation of *EC*.

NOTES

1 Eve Kosofsky Sedgwick, *Epistemology of the Closet* (Berkeley: University of California Press, 1990), xv.

2 Sedgwick, *Epistemology*, 1.

3 Sedgwick, *Epistemology*, 3.

4 Sedgwick, *Epistemology*, 32.

5 "Sedgwick Sense and Sensibility: An Interview with Eve Kosofsky Sedgwick," interview by Mark Kerr and Kristin O'Rourke, c 1995, http://nideffer.net/proj/Tvc/interviews/20.Tvc.v9.intrvws.Sedg.html.

6 Sedgwick, *Epistemology*, 1.

7 Sedgwick, *Epistemology*, 1.

8 Sedgwick, *Epistemology*, 22.

SECTION 1
INFLUENCES

MODULE 1
THE AUTHOR AND THE
HISTORICAL CONTEXT

KEY POINTS

- *Epistemology of the Closet* remains an important force in the dynamic and evolving field of Queer Theory.

- Sedgwick was a poet and artist as well as a literary scholar.

- One of the most significant aspects of the historical backdrop to the writing of *Epistemology of The Closet* was the personal and cultural toll of the HIV/AIDS crisis.

Why Read This Text?

Epistemology of the Closet is considered highly original because it was the first text to provide a sustained critical model to illustrate how the creation and experience of virtually all aspects of modern life emerge from a dualistic homo/heterosexual understanding of sexuality. In this way, Sedgwick helped to lay the foundations for what would soon be called Queer Theory—a still highly influential, if sometimes controversial, interdisciplinary field. *Epistemology of The Closet* is a text that unpacks assumptions about how sexuality, and specifically the definitional split between gay/straight, relates to the broader culture. In particular, Sedgwick's analysis displaces the tendency to see homosexuality as something that affects only a segment of the population. Sedgwick insists that the very idea that certain acts and people can be grouped into either/or, gay/straight categories structures the broader epistemological fabric of modern culture. The proliferation of gay rights around issues such as same-sex marriage, adoption, and military service since the book's publication in 1990

15

> **❝** So resilient and productive a structure of narrative [as the closet] will not readily surrender its hold on important forms of social meaning. **❞**
>
> Eve Kosofsky Sedgwick, *Epistemology of the Closet*

does not dampen its critical and political relevance because much of this progress relies on the strict cultural distinction between gay and straight that Sedgwick explores.

Author's Life

Eve Kosofsky was born on May 2, 1950, in Dayton Ohio. From an early age, Eve demonstrated an interest in scholarly pursuits as well as poetry and art. When her family moved to Bethesda, MD, near Washington, DC, she continued to excel academically and creatively. Here Eve was drawn to the theatrical milieu of Washington, which she credits with her awakening awareness of and attraction to a gay sensibility. Later, as a student at Cornell University, Eve met her husband Hal Sedgwick, whom she married in the summer of 1969. After completing her PhD at Yale, Sedgwick pursued a postdoctoral fellowship at Cornell University, and then various faculty positions in the United States before accepting tenure at Amherst College. By the time of accepting a full professorship at Duke University in 1988, Sedgwick had developed a reputation as an emerging, but also controversial, academic star.

With the publication of *Epistemology of The Closet* in 1990 Sedgwick continued to be a target of criticism. "Traditionalist" critics such as Hilton Kramer and Roger Kimball argue that the institutionalization of fields such as women studies, lesbian and gay studies,* and critical race studies, which Sedgwick was helping to shape at the time, was a betrayal of the principles of Western liberal arts. Sedgwick met this criticism with ambivalence and wit. She would later write that she felt she had little choice in this regard. This was because, during the height of the backlash in the early 1990s, Sedgwick was diagnosed with breast cancer. "The timing of the diagnosis couldn't have been better," she would later write, "if I'd needed a reminder I had one that, sure enough, life *is* too short, at least mine is, for going head-to-head with people whose highest approbation, even, would offer no intellectual or moral support."

In 1998, after the recurrence of this cancer, Sedgwick moved to New York to receive care and to be nearer to Hal. While teaching at CUNY, Sedgwick pursued writing and art vociferously, and traveled to Asia a number of times to satisfy a growing interest in Buddhism and in search of materials and inspiration for her expanding art practice. Although Sedgwick may be best known as an academic, her scholarship bears the deep imprint of her life as an artist, poet, and activist. Sedgwick died of breast cancer in New York in 2009.

Author's Background

In the preface to the 2008 edition of *Epistemology of The Closet*, Sedgwick names a number of elements forming the historical context behind its culmination. Having grown up in a Jewish family after World War II, the resistance to McCarthyism,* the civil rights movement,* and the student protests of the late sixties each played an important role in the exploration of what she calls the "closet dynamics" explored in the text. Of particular significance in this regard, however, is the interrelated issues of the American AIDS emergency and renewed expressions of homophobia at the highest levels of the American legal and political structure. The devastation of the initial AIDS epidemic in the United States made a powerful imprint on the scholarship and political activism of the time. "The intense dread of that period," Sedgwick writes, "included the political fear that AIDS phobia and the attendant sex panic would offer a pretext on which the entire society might be stripped of its liberties."[1] The trauma wrought by HIV/AIDS during the 1980s was compounded by openly anti-gay legislation (most notably the US Supreme Court decision in the case Bowers v. Hardwick [1986] to uphold a Georgian anti-sodomy law), as well as the equally telling inaction on the part of the federal government to address the AIDS crisis. Infamously, amidst rampant death, then-president Ronald Reagan* refused to even utter the word "AIDS" until many years into the epidemic.

NOTES

1   Eve Kosofsky Sedgwick, *Epistemology of the Closet* (Berkeley: University of California Press, 1990), xv.

MODULE 2
ACADEMIC CONTEXT

KEY POINTS

- *Epistemology of the Closet* reflects an intervention in the ways of reading the traditional canons of American and European literature.

- Sedgwick brought the question of homo/heterosexual definition to bear on many canonical Western texts of literary criticism.

- Sedgwick builds upon, but also revises, Michel Foucault's work on the relationship between power, discourse, and sexual identity.

The Work in its Context

Epistemology of the Closet was published at a time of flux and tension in the Humanities. The so-called culture wars*—partly a backlash to the advances of second wave* feminism* in the preceding decade—refers to debates over the alleged displacement of the traditional canon* of Western culture by a new focus on questions of identity and political justice. At the same time, the late eighties saw the popularization of theoretically-orientated forms of literary analysis at the highest levels of the academy. French poststructuralist theorists such as Michel Foucault and Jacques Derrida were becoming fixtures of the intellectual landscape in the United States. However, some literary critics saw this turn to "theory," and the institutionalization of fields such as women's studies, gay and lesbian studies, and cultural studies* as eroding traditional values of literary criticism and, indeed, of Western civilization itself. Thus, the context of *Epistemology of The Closet* was one in which the core concerns of literary criticism were, in large part,

> ❝ The relation of gay studies to debates on the literary
> canon is, and had best be, torturous. ❞
>
> Eve Kosofsky Sedgwick, *Epistomology of the Closet*

self-reflexive. The field was deeply enmeshed in debates over questions such as: what kinds of texts are legitimate subjects for literary analysis? What kinds of questions should we ask of literature? And what should we make, if anything, of a text's political and historical context?

Overview of the Field

Sedgwick's work can be seen as both coming out of and helping to precipitate the emergence of cultural studies and theoretical approaches such as deconstruction* within the literary academy. Rather than seeking to expand the field of literary criticism to include "gay texts" as a supplement to the traditional canon, Sedgwick instead brought the question of homosexuality to bear on established texts of literary criticism. In this way, Sedgwick helped to disrupt the safe line of demarcation between traditional literary criticism on the one hand, and gay and lesbian studies on the other. This disruption was controversial. Some rightwing commentators were appalled at the notion that homosexuality could be taught on a mainstream curriculum alongside Plato and Shakespeare. In 1990, *News Week* for example, lamented that universities were not only welcoming homosexuals but mandating the study of gay culture as well. In response to this "political correctness" scare piece, Sedgwick offered the following retort: "Read any Sonnets lately? You dip into the Phaedrus often? To invoke the utopian bedroom scene of Chuck Berry's immortal aubade: Roll over, Beethoven, and tell Tchaikovsky the news."[1] What Sedgwick is saying here, in a slightly sarcastic way, is that the Western canon of literature was already *plenty* gay before anyone like her came along to "mandate" it.

Academic Influences

Sedgwick was influenced by many schools of thought including feminist theory, poststructuralism, deconstruction, and Marxism.* Indeed, much of the originality of Sedgwick's work is due to her ability to move productively between these various paradigms of thinking. As a student at Cornell and Yale during the 1970s, Sedgwick was exposed not only to New Criticism's preoccupation with close reading, but also the French literary theories such as deconstruction that were being popularized in the academy at the time. The French post-structuralist critic Michel Foucault* is perhaps the most notable influence on Sedgwick's work. Foucault examines how power is constituted through systems of naming and categorizing. Sedgwick's *Between Men* (1985) and *Epistemology of The Closet* can be seen as a reappraisal of Foucault's thesis on how the historical and discursive development of sexuality as a system of medical, legal cultural categorization comes to form the ways bodies are disciplined socially.

Sedgwick's ideas are often read in parallel with the work of another foundational thinker of her generation, Judith Butler.* Both authors are grounded in Feminist schools of thought and their writing focuses on "performativity"—a concept adapted through readings of J. L. Austin* (1911–60), a British philosopher of language. Together, the work of Butler and Sedgwick can be seen as laying much of the theoretical foundations for a school of thought that, from the 1990s, would be called Queer Theory.

NOTES

1   Eve Kosofsky Sedgwick, *Tendencies* (Durham: Routledge, 1994), 20.

MODULE 3
THE PROBLEM

KEY POINTS

- Sedgwick's core question is how does the homo/hetero-sexual definition structure modern epistemologies?

- Sedgwick's key problem is how modern culture is produced by the unstable distinction between homosexuality and heterosexuality.

- And she builds on and reorients important work by Michel Foucault, who argues that discourse and power are inextricably intertwined.

Core Question

While the "issue" of homosexuality and homophobia were a part of public and political discourse at the time of *Epistemology of the Closet*'s publication, Sedgwick's objective was to complicate their relationship to modern structures of knowledge (epistemologies) more broadly. The concept of "the closet" refers to the metaphorical hidden space in which non-heterosexuals suppress their same-sex desire or live out their desire only in secrecy, while fearing persecution should that desire or sexual activity be exposed. In Western culture, this state of partial or total secrecy regarding one's sexuality is known as "the closet." This basic understanding of the closet is examined and complicated by Sedgwick in *Epistemology of The Closet* . In particular, she considers how the homo/heterosexual binary configures the "closet relations" of modern epistemologies, even those that seemingly have nothing to do with homosexuality, or even sexuality itself. Through her readings of literature, Sedgwick complicates our "common sense" understanding of sexuality. The distinction

> ❝ Among the questions asked by *Epistemology of the Closet is how we*, thinking from one fleeting historical moment, can wrap our minds properly around the mix of immemorial, seemingly fixed discourses of sexuality and, at the same time, around discourses that may be much more recent, ephemeral, contingent. ❞
>
> Eve Kosofsky Sedgwick, "2008 Preface," *Epistemology of the Closet*

between gay and straight may seems intuitive, but in fact, there is nothing common sense or predetermined about those two categories. Instead, this binary opposition comes out of a particular history, and works in subtle, albeit powerful, ways to structure our knowledge of society and the world more broadly in such ways that limit freedom and understanding. With this argument, Sedgwick counters positivist* ideologies that frame homosexuality as something with a straightforward (e.g., biological or societal) "cause."

The Participants

The participants of the debate that *Epistemology of The Closet* engages in may not be other academics so much as different common sense and institutionally held views about sexuality. For example, at the time of *Epistemology of The Closet*'s publication, like today, it was common—from both pro-gay and anti-gay perspectives—to see homosexuality as a fundamentally distinct category of sexuality, which thus corresponded to an equally distinct category of gay culture. Sedgwick's analysis disrupts this belief, insisting that the distinction between gay and straight is something that runs to the very core of modern thought. As a result, there can be no clear demarcation between what is homo- or heterosexual. If contemporary knowledge and power relations are formed out of the conceptual distinction between gay/

straight, then it becomes impossible to say that something (or someone) is strictly one or the other.

The other key participant in the debate is Judith Butler, whose book *Gender Trouble* (published the same year as *Epistemology of The Closet*), complements Sedgwick's work in many ways and is likewise seen as helping to lay the foundations of Queer Theory. In *Gender Trouble,* Butler complicates the received distinction between gender and sex, where gender is understood as a socially constructed set of norms and sex is understood as an innately biological determinant. Butler argues that sex, too, is contingent on a particular discursive and social history such that it exercises power (in both enabling and disabling ways) differently for different people. Thus, just as Butler challenges essentialist and biologically determinist frameworks of understanding gender expression and experience, so too does Sedgwick challenge these frameworks with respect to sexuality. To make their respective claims, both authors draw upon and adapt the work of the philosopher J. L. Austin and the concept of the performative utterance or "performativity." Performativity refers to the notion that speaking not only describes the world, but changes the conditions of social reality. This idea is important to both Butler and Sedgwick because it allows them to reach beyond the belief that gender and sexuality are simply static things "out there" naturally in the world waiting to be named.

The Contemporary Debate

Sedgwick presents a history of sexuality that is both a modification and an elaboration of Michel Foucault's groundbreaking text *The History of Sexuality*, which charts the development of homosexuality as a clinical category in order to explore the roots of modern power in medical discourse. Like Foucault, Sedgwick was interested in thinking about homosexuality as something culturally constructed, which is to say historically and contextually specific. In particular,

Sedgwick sought to complicate what she saw as the limitations around the either-or debate as to whether homosexuality should be understood as the product of natural forces such as DNA, or of an individual's social and cultural environment. To approach this nature vs. culture debate from a fresh vantage point, Sedgwick recasts it in terms of what she calls minoritizing and universalizing logics. Sedgwick defines a minoritizing logic as "seeing homo/heterosexual definition ... as an issue of active importance primarily for a small, distinct, relatively fixed homosexual minority."[1] An example of the minoritizing logic is the idea of the "gay gene" that suggests that some people have, embedded in their very biology, the making of homosexual identity while others do not. By contrast, she defines the universalizing logic as that which sees homosexuality as a kind of "solvent" that moves right through the culture.[2] An example of the universalizing logic is the notion of the gay spectrum—i.e., the belief that "everyone is at least a little gay." Sedgwick observes that these two logics, while seemingly incompatible, do in fact coexist in our culture. This coexistence, Sedgwick argues, produces a kind of cultural double-bind incoherence with respect to the closet. Because the limits of homosexuality are unstable, each new relationship and social scenario brings with it new dynamics of potential revelation and secrecy. Thus, the closet cannot be understood as something of which one is strictly "in" or "out".

That being said, it is not Sedgwick's aim to resolve this incoherence or to otherwise pick a side as to whether the minoritizing or universalizing logic is correct; rather, her goal is to lay out feelers for how this unresolved tension permeates and affects the culture. Through her readings of literature, Sedgwick shows how our "common sense" understanding of sexuality is built on very uncommon-sense tensions and contradictions. If one of the questions that Michel Foucault asks in *The History of Sexuality* is, how is the idea of homosexuality invented *vis*-a-vis modern discourse, then in a sense, what Sedgwick does is ask the inverse. That is to say, how does the homo/heterosexual definition itself structure the epistemology* of culture?

NOTES

1   Eve Kosofsky Sedgwick, *Epistemology of the Closet* (Berkeley: University of California Press, 1990), 1.

2   Sedgwick, *Epistemology,* 85.

MODULE 4
THE AUTHOR'S CONTRIBUTION

KEY POINTS

- *Epistemology of the Closet* aims to develop a critical paradigm of homosexuality beyond the coarse explanation of same-sex attraction.

- Sedgwick explores both how a binary understanding of homo/heterosexuality configures the broader culture.

- Sedgwick's work in *Epistemology of The Closet* both builds on and reframes the questions asked by Michel Foucault in his groundbreaking text, *The History of Sexuality*.

Author's Aims

One of the stated aims of *Epistemology of the Closet* is to develop a sexuality-centered paradigm of scholarly criticism. This was intended as a complement to the feminist scholarship that focuses largely on the axis of gender (man v. woman). Sedgwick seeks to demonstrate that the binary between homo/heterosexual definition is at least as significant to modern culture as the dichotomy between man and woman. The book itself is organized less as a step-by-step thesis than as a series of essays linked by their shared themes and questions. Broadly speaking, the book can be broken down into three interrelated parts. First, in the introduction, Sedgwick situates the "project in the larger context of gay/lesbian and antihomophobic theory."[1] Second, in chapter one, she outlines the overarching thesis of the project—namely that the homo/heterosexual definition is a premising dichotomy rather than simply one outcome of modern, Western thought. Chapters 2 and 3 unpack this thesis further by testing it against a broad set of "binarized cultural nexuses," such as knowledge/

> 66 I think that a whole cluster of the most crucial sites for the contestation of meaning in twentieth-century Western culture are consequentially and quite indelibly marked with the historical specificity of homosocial/homosexual definition. 99
>
> Eve Kosofsky Sedgwick, *Epistemology of the Closet*

ignorance and natural/unnatural.[2] Thirdly, in the final section of the book (chapters 4 and 5), Sedgwick applies the critical framework developed throughout the preceding chapters outwards to real-life experience. Here the focus in on the notion of "homosexual panic" (chapter 4), and the performative dimensions of the closet and the act of "coming out" (chapter 5).

Approach

Sedgwick's approach to studying homosexuality is somewhat counterintuitive. Whereas many from Foucault onwards have sought to explore how homosexuality is culturally constructed by modern relations of knowledge and power, in a sense Sedgwick explores this relationship in reverse. For Sedgwick the question is not how does modern society produce the idea of homosexuality so much as how does the homo/heterosexual definition produce the modern culture for all its complexity, contradiction, and ambiguities?

In reframing the question of homosexuality in that way, Sedgwick offers an innovative reframing of the social constructionism* prevalent in Queer Theory to this day. Sedgwick also departs in major ways from the mainstream lesbian and gay political framing of homosexuality. Rather than understanding homosexuality as a distinct identity separate from heterosexuality, as mainstream lesbian and gay politics tends to, Sedgwick seeks to prove that the homo/heterosexual distinction is a matter of complexities, tensions, and contradictions that cannot be easily identified let alone relegated to a specific corner of society. For Sedgwick, the establishment of sexual identity, far from resolving contradictions and ambiguities, is the very thing that exposes us to them. For example, Sedgwick shows how the "nature" and "nurture" explanations of the "cause" of homosexuality (i.e., whether homosexuality is the result of biological or cultural factors) coexist in our understanding of gay identity, despite being essentially contradictory in nature. Of the nature v. nurture debate, Sedgwick writes: "the performative effects of the self-contradictory discursive field of force created by their overlap will be my subject."[3] In drawing out these contradictions and complexities it was partially Sedgwick's aim to undo the damaging effects of a culture that seemed to refuse to recognize its own (homo)sexual attachments, as well as how those attachments defy any clean dualist logic of homo/heterosexual identity.

Sedgwick approaches her core question through a literary frame, exploring how the homo/heterosexual binary is mapped out, often ambiguously, in texts that may or may not have a conventionally explicit homosexual theme or subject matter. The authors Sedgwick reads in *Epistemology of The Closet* include Herman Melville,* Oscar Wilde,* Nietzsche,* Henry James,* and Proust,* suggesting that Sedgwick did not reject the canon wholesale. Her critique was more a question of how to engage the canon. Thus, Sedgwick forges a kind of queer intimacy between the traditional canon of English literature and poststructuralist methodologies to imagine new avenues of thinking in and around feminist and gay studies.

Contribution in Context

Perhaps the most notable intellectual contexts in which *Epistemology of The Closet* intervenes is that of the French philosopher Michel Foucault. In 1978 the introductory volume of *The History of Sexuality* was translated into English, and as it gained recognition in the Anglo-

American context, it profoundly shaped the way people thought about the relationship between power and knowledge, and between history and identity. Broadly speaking, Foucault argued that, rather that suppressing or censuring sexuality, the effect of power is to *produce* it. For Foucault, power is closely enmeshed with discursive knowledge. The discourse that we use to describe who we are—labels, names, measurements, categories, identities, and so on—is the very thing that secures us to systems of state power. *Epistemology of The Closet* builds on and deepens this observation, homing in on the way homo/heterosexual definition informs other categories of meaning and thus disciplinary power itself. Thus, Sedgwick's contribution has a lot to do with her ability to engage with the vanguard of postmodernism* that was gaining roots during the 1980s and '90s. Indeed, much of the recognition *Epistemology of The Closet* received at the time of its publication was due to the sensitivity and skill with which it employs the methods of continental philosophy—namely deconstruction and poststructuralism.* Sedgwick not only borrowed from these methods, she also helped to reshape them by showing how they were deeply relevant to political questions of both personal and societal importance in an American context.

NOTES

1   Eve Kosofsky Sedgwick, *Epistemology of the Closet* (Berkeley: University of California Press, 1990), 12.

2   Sedgwick, *Epistemology,* 12.

3   Sedgwick, *Epistemology,* 9.

SECTION 2
IDEAS

MAIN IDEAS

KEY POINTS

- The key themes of *Epistemology of the Closet* involve what Sedgwick calls "the potent incoherences of homo/heterosexual definition."

- These incoherences themselves underpin the broader cultural dynamics of society.

- As with other scholars working in a deconstructive style, play with language is central to Sedgwick's intellectual project.

Key Themes

In *Epistemology of the Closet*, Sedgwick argues, "homosexual definition"—that is to say, the epistemological distinction that divides people into a gay/straight dichotomy—"is organized around a radical and irreducible incoherence."[1] Sedgwick highlights the myriad and complicated ways both heterosexual and homosexual attachments depend on structures of kinship and intimacy that do not match up neatly with gender attraction or sexual "orientation," *per se*. There are two thematic tensions that inform Sedgwick's broader thesis. The first has do with the coexistence of the minoritizing and universalizing logics around homosexuality. Once again, the minoritizing logic of homosexuality is the belief that homosexuality is something that affects a distinct minority of individuals within the broader society, while the universalizing logic is the belief that homosexuality is something that exists at a broad societal level and thus affects people regardless of their particular sexual preferences. Crucially, the point Sedgwick makes about the minoritizing and universalizing logics of

> ❝ An understanding of virtually any aspect of modern Western culture must be, not merely incomplete, but damaged in its central substance to the degree that it does not incorporate a critical analysis of the modern homo/heterosexual definition. ❞
>
> Eve Kosofsky Sedgwick, *Epistemology of the Closet*

homosexuality is not that one is right and one wrong. Instead, Sedgwick argues that these seemingly incompatible perspectives on homosexuality can and do coexist simultaneously, and that contemporary culture then emerges out of this incoherence. In other words, what Sedgwick observes is that it is neither the minoritizing logic (nature) nor the universalizing logic (culture) that determines the epistemology of the closet. Rather, the epistemology of the closet is the very sense that homosexuality is somehow both everywhere all around us and isolated to a minority of the population. This leads to a kind of anxiety (and phobia) in our culture about where heterosexuality ends and homosexuality begins.

This notion of anxiety about the "proper" shape and boundary of homosexuality brings us to the second major theme of the book, namely the dualism between disclosure and secrecy that constitutes the idea of the gay closet. The closet refers to the act of hiding one's homosexuality while other people's sexuality is putatively visible. At its face, the notion of the closet suggests that some people are open about their sexuality while others are not. But as Sedgwick explores at length in *Epistemology of The Closet,* the divisions between knowing and not knowing, visibility and secrecy, freedom and closetedness as they pertain to homosexuality, are far messier than we might think (and hope) it to be. A good example of this complexity is the US military policy "Don't Ask, Don't Tell."* This official US policy (1994-2011) meant that gay women and men could serve in the military with the understanding that no one would inquire about their sexuality on the condition that they themselves did not disclose it. What this policy reflects quite clearly is what Sedgwick calls "the reign of the telling secret."[2] By stating that the US military would not acknowledge homosexuality in its ranks, it was acknowledging homosexuality in its ranks. This example reflects both the incoherence of the closet as a complex of overlapping forms of knowing and not knowing, as well as the overlapping interplay of the minoritizing and universalizing logics of homosexuality, two themes that underwrite Sedgwick's broader project about the way homo/heterosexual definition saturates our culture.

Exploring the Ideas

For Sedgwick, these two themes—the "spectacle of the closet," and the intertwined dynamic of the minoritizing and universalizing logics of homosexuality—exemplify the incoherence and ambiguity that comes out of the homo/heterosexual definition, but they also inform relations and identities far beyond the explicit purview of sexual orientation. Although Sedgwick develops this thesis predominantly through readings of literary texts, it is worth reflecting further on how these two main themes/incoherences relate to the real-world dynamics of sexuality that is the true subject of her analysis. How do the ways we define homosexuality structure not only our ideas about sexuality but also broader forms of social power and exclusion?

For one, Sedgwick sees the minoritizing logic—even when coming from liberal or "pro-gay" sources—as dangerous because it Epistemology of The Closet hoes the purifying impulse behind the desire to categorize people. In other words, the idea that homosexuality has a positivist (genetic) cause is never far removed, in Sedgwick's mind, from the fantasy that it is something that can ultimately be corrected or eliminated. In *Epistemology of The Closet, ,* Sedgwick confronts the idea that removing the cause of homosexuality might be justified in the name of social cohesion. For Sedgwick, homosexuality is not something with a discrete cause, but a sensibility that runs through culture in complex ways. While her inclination is towards a more universalizing view of homosexuality, she acknowledges that it too is fraught with danger. For example, to say that homosexuality is something that runs through the culture may risk flattening what is distinct about queer people, queer experiences, queer things, and queer ideas. The key here is that the perpetual jockeying between the universalizing and minimizing logics produces a kind of anxiety around the fact that it is ultimately impossible to draw a firm line between homosexuality and heterosexuality; they are mutually constitutive categories. Thus, if it is impossible to demarcate the line between gay and straight in any clear fashion, we begin to see how complicated it becomes for society to insist upon, as it does, the liberation of gay people based on their freedom to come out of the closet. If the events of Stonewall* and the subsequent gay liberation and gay rights movements* brought with them a new impetus for gays to be open about their sexuality, it also inserted them into an increasingly layered drama of secrecy and disclosure.

The birth of the gay rights movement was hardly a moment to dispense with the closet. As Sedgwick writes, "so resilient and productive a structure of narrative will not readily surrender its hold on important forms of social meaning."[3] A different way of putting this would be to say that the increased visibility of homosexuality in the latter part the twentieth century brought to the fore new forms of sexual invisibility. Thus, the closet dynamics that Sedgwick explores begs several questions: What does it mean to be "out" exactly? To everyone? At all times? In all circumstances? Furthermore, given that Sedgwick saw theses contradictions and questions as deeply connected to structures of exclusion, it is also worth asking for whom does the logic of the closet work most beneficially? And who benefits from, not just being "out," but from the very idea that there is "in" and "out"? Does being out as a white middle class gay man married to another white middle class gay man mean the same thing as being out as a working-class person of color? Does it mean the same thing as being out as a woman in a heterosexual relationship who also has sex with women? These and similar questions help us see how the epistemology of the closet functions differently for different people, and how it helps to structure intersectional relations of power across class, race, and gender.

Language and Expression

Epistemology of The Closet is often regarded as a "difficult" text. Partly owing to its deconstructionist approach, Sedgwick's writing style tends to be highly complex, employing specialist terms, and dense and long sentences. Sedgwick was fond of the list as a form of writing, often used neologisms, and worked deliberately to expand and complicate the meanings of words. In this regard Sedgwick's work is experimental, both in style and content. In relation to the perception of the book as difficult, however, it is crucial to recognize that Sedgwick's work was never intended as a crystalline composition of sequential theories and concepts, but as a living text that might share some critical, creative and subjective connections with the reader's own intellectual and emotional process. Understanding the inherent subjectivity of any reading experience is an important part of understanding Sedgwick's work. Like other postmodernist scholars, Sedgwick rejects the idea that a text has an authoritative meaning implanted in it by its author and subsequently deciphered by the reader, either correctly or wrongly. But for a text that is rigorously analytical, Sedgwick's writing is also textured and playful. Sedgwick was fond of puns and list form in her writing, and never shied away from using innuendo to bring out the erotic or political significance of literary texts. These qualities foreshadow the more personal tones of her later work.

NOTES

1   Eve Kosofsky Sedgwick, *Epistemology of the Closet* (Berkeley: University of California Press, 1990), 67.

2   Sedgwick, 67.

3   Sedgwick, 67.

SECONDARY IDEAS

KEY POINTS

- Sedgwick argues that the study of (homo)sexual definition requires a sexuality-based paradigm distinct from the question of sex (i.e., gender).

- Sedgwick's framing thus has important disciplinary distinctions from feminist theory.

- *Epistemology of the Closet*, however, is still relevant to lesbians and women more broadly.

Other Ideas

Sedgwick organizes the introduction to *Epistemology of the Closet* as a series of axioms, which highlight a number of ideas that support the overall thesis of the book. One of these axioms is the argument that sex and gender, while related, are not coextensive. Sedgwick acknowledges that there can be no concept of homosexuality without there first being a concept of gender (after all homosexuality means, quite simply, the attraction to one's own gender). But the axis of gender is also fundamentally limited, Sedgwick argues, because there are many dimensions to sexuality that have little to do with gender, such as age, power, position, and the variety of sexual acts themselves. This axiom is central to Sedgwick's broader thesis because it allows her to insist on the need for a method and framework for thinking of homosexuality beyond the rubric of gender alone. Another one of these axioms is that "there can't be a priori decision about how far it will make sense to conceptualize lesbian and gay male identities together. Or separately."[1] Here, Sedgwick acknowledges that her own work focuses specifically on male homosexuality. She also observes the

> ❝ The question of gender and the question of sexuality, inextricable from one another though they are in that each can be expressed only in terms of the other, are nonetheless not the same question ❞
>
> Eve Kosofsky Sedgwick, *Epistemology of the Closet*

historical tendency for women's sexual, and specifically homosexual, experience to be subsumed by men's. Accepting this, however, Sedgwick does not concede that a specifically male-centered analysis of homo/heterosexual definition will not have value to a specifically lesbian theoretical project. No doubt lesbian experience bears a different relationship to the patriarchal society, but for Sedgwick it is equally important to note "the many ways in which male and female homosexual identity [have] in fact been constructed through and in relation to each other."[2]

Exploring the Ideas

Sedgwick's axiom about the tensions between the axes of gender and sexuality is worth further reflection. Sedgwick's argument is that the axis of gender is insufficiently equipped for exploring the nuances and complexity of homosexuality. That is to say, there is a lot more to homosexuality than simply same-sex attraction. This has serious consequences for how Sedgwick sees her work in relation to the work of her academic peers. Sedgwick advocates for at least a partial split between gender studies and gay and lesbian studies, and between feminist enquiry and sexuality studies. "Antihomophobic inquiry," Sedgwick writes, "is not coextensive with feminist inquiry. But we can't know in advance how they will be different."[3] Although she does not use the term, it is here that Sedgwick effectively calls Queer Theory into being. Sedgwick argues that thinking through the axis of sexuality has the possibility of revealing different dynamics of oppression, identity, and power that feminist theorizing might otherwise take for granted. This is due in part to what Sedgwick refers to as the superior deconstructive potential of the heterosexual/homosexual binary in comparison to the dichotomy male/female. For Sedgwick, the binary of male/female remains so calcified in culture that it affords less "potential for rearrangement, ambiguity, and representational doubleness" then the relation of heterosexual/homosexual.[4] Thus, by calling for a specifically sexuality-based framework, with this axiom, Sedgwick provides a justification of her own analysis of the minoritizing/universalizing logics of homosexuality and the dynamics of concealment and revelation that attend the figure of the gay closet. Neither of these inherences would be parsed using the rubric of gender or same-sex attraction alone.

Overlooked

Perhaps the most neglected aspect of *Epistemology of The Closet* is its utility to lesbian-feminist research. Because of the text's primary focus on the same-sex bonds between men, *Epistemology of The Closet,* as with Sedgwick's work in general, has been accused of being irrelevant to women's studies and lesbian scholarship.[5] Indeed, the relationship between feminist research and Queer Theory continues to be a contentious issue within the humanities, many arguing that the latter, which Sedgwick helped to establish, obfuscates the power relations between women and men in order to produce a universal "queer" category. Others, however, have argued that Sedgwick's relevance to lesbian studies has been either denied or overlooked.[6] Thus the relevance of *Epistemology of The Closet* to feminist research and lesbian studies is ripe for reconsideration and reinterpretation.

Because the overriding thesis of *Epistemology of The Closet* can be readily summarized in one or two sentences, aspects that do not directly pertain to this overarching thesis tend to be overlooked. As such, linking less prominent aspects of the text to lines of inquiry that

40

emerge in Sedgwick's later work (such as affect theory* and Buddhist pedagogies) has been and will continue to be a meaningful way of reinterpreting *Epistemology of The Closet*. Indeed, Sedgwick was herself weary of the way texts could grow stagnant within their own field of study. In *Epistemology of The Closet* and elsewhere, Sedgwick reads canonical texts, not to establish new definitive interpretations, but rather to destabilize their taken-for-granted meanings. For the noted queer theorist Lauren Berlant,* Sedgwick was someone who could help you "appreciate being wobbly in knowledge."[7] That invitation into uncertainty is a powerful reminder to Sedgwick's readers to approach *Epistemology of The Closet* as something contingent, unfinished, and evolving.

NOTES

1   Eve Kosofsky Sedgwick, *Epistemology of the Closet* (Berkeley: University of California Press, 1990), 36.

2   Sedgwick, 37.

3   Sedgwick, 27.

4   Sedgwick, 34.

5   See: Blakey Vermeule, "Is There a Sedgwick School for Girls?," *Qui Parle* 5, no. 1 (1991): 53–72. And Terry Castle, *The Apparitional Lesbian: Female Homosexuality and Modern Culture* (New York: Columbia University Press, 1993).

6   See: Jason Edwards, *Eve Kosofsky Sedgwick* (London: Routledge, 2009), 145.

7   Lauren Berlant, "Eve Sedgwick, Once More," *Critical Inquiry* 35, 2009: 1089–91.

MODULE 7
ACHIEVEMENT

KEY POINTS

- At the time of its publication, *Epistemology of the Closet* had a significant impact in changing how scholars approached questions of sexuality, identity, and power.

- Sedgwick's work received significant backlash from conservative cultural commentators.

- Outside the academy, Sedgwick's arguments are not commonplace.

Assessing the Argument

In many ways, Sedgwick, in *Epistemology of the Closet*, was extremely successful in achieving her stated aims. Along with Judith Butler's *Gender Trouble,* she helped set in motion the analytic model of Queer Theory, thus realizing her ambition of developing a critical framework informed by, but also separate from, the feminist axis of gender. At the time of its publication, *Epistemology of The Closet* was highly regarded as a ground-breaking intervention in literary criticism and continues to shape the meanings and directions of sexuality studies to this day. This is not to say that Sedgwick did not receive resistance or that she saw her own ideas as fully realized in *Epistemology of The Closet*. Indeed, Sedgwick describes *Tendencies*, published in 1994, as taking up what she failed to get to in *Epistemology of The Closet*.

The task of assessing the influence of Sedgwick's work *beyond* the academy is immeasurably more difficult. It would perhaps be a leap to say that Sedgwick's anti-homophobic criticism brought about any kind of paradigm shift in the broader culture. That being said, Sedgwick was, in fact, suspicious of the very idea of paradigm shifts.

> ❝[Sedgwick] changed for a generation of scholars and activists ... how we think about the nexus of identity, desires, bodies, prohibition, discourses, and the play of power.❞
>
> Stephen M. Barber and David L. Clark, "Queer Moments: The Performative Temporalities of Eve Kosofsky Sedgwick"

In *Epistemology of The Closet* she suggests that thinking about homosexuality in terms of monumental shifts in attitudes obscure the ways sexuality is lived out. This is because, for Sedgwick, the question of what our cultural "attitude" to homosexuality is in the first place is never settled. Homosexuality designates the very place where contradictions such as desire and disgust, power and vulnerability, love and hatred collide.

Achievement in Context

The 1990s, the decade that immediately followed the publication of *Epistemology of The Closet*, was a period that brought about new forms of homosexual visibility in the Anglo-American context. It was a period in which the AIDS emergency continued to play itself out, but also a period in which advances in treatment profoundly changed what it meant to be HIV-positive for the better. It was a period in which the violence faced by gay people gained nation-wide exposure following the murder of Matthew Shepard,* an event that received unprecedented media attention. And it was a period that saw gay rights discourses coalesce around issues like the right to serve in the military, adopt children, and to marry. These and other shifts in the broader culture may well explain the appetite that existed for *Epistemology of The Closet*. There was at the time, no doubt, a desire for new ways of thinking about the relationship between homosexuality and culture—both inside and outside the academy. It is important to note, however, that Sedgwick's work does not *explain* these shifts in the visibility of homosexuality, or prescribe fixes for their shortcomings. Sedgwick's primary interest was not in any kind of empirical diagnostics of culture and its problems. Instead, she helped to develop something like a critical lens that uses the homo/heterosexual split as a frame for thinking about the fluid and shifting patterns of cultural meaning.

In many respects Sedgwick was a victim of her own success. During the early nineties, many universities were in the process of institutionalizing the study of identity, race, gender, sexuality, and so on within their curriculum. In this environment, Sedgwick was a rising star. As her notoriety grew, however, she also became the target of a reactionary move in the academy. Many inside and outside the academy viewed the changes taking place in the academy as an attack on the very fabric of the Western culture; Sedgwick was singled out as one of the instigators of these changes. In this environment, however, she was targeted not so much for what she said in her scholarship, as for what she seemed to represent.

Limitations

Although *Epistemology of The Closet* remains a foundational text for scholars of gender and sexuality studies, and Queer Theory, there is much less evidence to suggest that Sedgwick's arguments have penetrated into mainstream discourse. Notably, in both conservative and progressive/liberal circles, contemporary identity politics continues to perpetuate what Sedgwick calls a minoritizing logic, whereby homosexuality is understood as something innate to certain people, and often biologically determined. We can think, for example, of the moniker "born this way," which circulates in liberal gay culture. In this climate, gayness is understood as something one is born with and that is indelible. Sedgwick observes a strange and potentially dangerous closeness between this brand of the minoritizing logic and normative discourses that disavow the ambiguity and fluidity of sexual experience and bolsters regulatory ideas about sexual classification. To say that people are born one way or another—*either* straight or gay, normal or queer—is to ignore the mutually constituted relationship between homosexuality and heterosexuality. In this sense, then, Sedgwick's work, and Queer Theory in general, remains overshadowed by ideas about sexuality that are often passed off as "common sense," but that in fact obscure the inherent incoherences of homo/heterosexual definition.

MODULE 8
PLACE IN THE AUTHOR'S WORK

KEY POINTS

- *Epistemology of the Closet* forms, in many respects, the centerpiece of Sedgwick's professional life.

- It builds on the theme of male-male relations established in her earlier work and foreshadows later preoccupations in queerness and affect.

- *EC* is widely regarded as Sedgwick's most influential work.

Positioning

Sedgwick's intellectual trajectory can be described as a move from a focus on specifically male same-sex reactions (*Between Men* [1985], and *Epistemology of the Closet* [1990]) towards an interest in the subtler register of affect, and a more expansive frame of queerness (*A Dialogue on Love* [1999], *Touching Feeling* [2003]), with *Tendencies* (1993) working as a kind of bridge in between. Thus, *Epistemology of The Closet* can be positioned within Sedgwick's work as a text that helped establish the terms of her life-long project of investigating the tensions between meaning and sexuality, but also a launching pad for directions and preoccupations that could hardly have been anticipated in 1990. It is perhaps worth noting, as well, that Sedgwick was diagnosed with cancer shortly after the publication of *Epistemology of The Closet*, and this no doubt had some influence in shaping the path of Sedgwick's subsequent work. At the very least, as Sedgwick writes in *Tendencies,* her diagnosis allowed her not to let herself become ensnared in the cynical criticisms she was facing at the time. It may also have something to do with a shift in the senses of urgency that characterized her earlier and later work. *Tendencies* concludes with a piece about friendship and

> 66 What I'm proudest of, I guess, is having a life where work and love are impossible to tell apart. 99
> Eve Kosofsky Sedgwick, *A Dialogue on Love*

mourning that is part autobiography and love letter. It is a piece that foreshadows, in many respects, *A Dialogue on Love* about her experience in therapy and what it means to *be* without fully *being* a "cancer patient." Both texts blur the lines of genre and are deeply attuned to the subtleties and ambiguities of feeling, affection, and desire.

Integration

The thrust of Sedgwick's work throughout her life can be seen not only as a cumulative trajectory, but also a kind of letting go. Sedgwick describes *Touching Feeling* as partly an account "of a writer's decreasing sense of having a strong center of gravity in a particular intellectual field."[1] The ungrounding that Sedgwick describes here speaks to a kind of openness that characterizes her later work—from the more interventionist mode of scholarship to something more textured, diffuse, and subtle. In *Touching Feeling*, Sedgwick describes her intention to write forms of criticism that, unlike her earlier work, would be less self-sure and less closed off from her various other creative practices, including editorial collaborations, poetry, memoir, cancer journalism, and nonlinguistic textile art. No doubt, for current readers, there is significant potential in studying *Epistemology of The Closet* in concert with not only her later academic work on affect and performativity, but also the other modes of creativity that she increasingly made time and energy for later in her life. What Sedgwick's later work lacks in an interventionist mode, it makes up for in a kind of openness and generosity, reflecting not only a new personal quality, but also a more accessible writing style. Despite this trajectory, however, it would be wrong to see Sedgwick's affective turn as anything other than a reflexive and critical continuation of earlier work. Taken collectively, Sedgwick's corpus reflects a deep, life-long interest in both the meanings of intimacy and the intimacies of thought.

Significance

Epistemology of The Closet is widely regarded as Sedgwick's most influential book—"the one that would not just turn heads but blow minds," as Ann Pellegrini describes in *The Chronicle of Higher Education*.[2] And it is widely regarded as a text that helped to inaugurate the interdisciplinary field of Queer Theory/studies. *Epistemology of The Closet* was Sedgwick's third book and one that, along with the easier *Between Men*, cemented her reputation as a rising star in the humanities. That being said, given the present-day academic focus on questions of affect, many new readers may come to Sedgwick via her later writing, which foregrounds questions of emotion, pedagogy, and expression, and is less interventionist in its posture. Nonetheless, *Epistemology of The Closet* remains, in most tellings, the centerpiece of Sedgwick's career. Even as her interests moved in various new directions to encapsulate affect, pedagogy, Buddhism, and memoir, her name remained synonymous with the foundation of Queer Theory, so such so that when the *New York Times* pronounced that "'Queer Theory' is Entering the Literary Mainstream"[3] in 1998, it was as the title of an article devoted to Sedgwick and her work.

NOTES

1 Eve Kosofsky Sedgwick, *Touching Feeling: Affect, Pedagogy, Performativity* (Durham: Duke UP, 2003), 2.

2 Ann Pellegrini, "Eve Kosofsky Sedgwick," *The Chronicle of Higher Education*, May 8, 2009, https://www.chronicle.com/article/Eve-Kosofsky-Sedgwick/15045.

3 Dinitia Smith, "'Queer Theory' Is Entering The Literary Mainstream," *The New York Times*, January 17, 1998, sec. Books, https://www.nytimes.com/1998/01/17/books/queer-theory-is-entering-the-literary-mainstream.html.

SECTION 3
IMPACT

MODULE 9
THE FIRST RESPONSES

KEY POINTS

- Much of the criticism levelled at Sedgwick had more to do with the institutionalization of cultural studies than with what she actually said.

- Some critics have argued that Sedgwick's understanding of the closet is disconnected from material realities of homosexual life.

- We see clear echoes between the backlash against Sedgwick's work in the 1990s and conservative critiques of the university today.

Criticism

Critiques of *Epistemology of the Closet* after its publication tended to focus less on the particularities of Sedgwick's arguments and more broadly on the legitimacy of cultural studies, and gender and sexuality studies as academic fields. Many viewed the emergence of cultural studies as a dangerous and ideologically-motivated distortion of literary criticism. As someone who employed the critical methods of poststructuralism and deconstruction, many perceived Sedgwick as an emblem of a misguided turn in the humanities. Perhaps the most frequently cited critic of Sedgwick's work is Roger Kimball. Kimball staunchly rejects the validity of both cultural studies and theories of poststructuralism that Sedgwick championed. Writing in *The New Criterion*, he describes Queer Theory and feminism among the many scourges of American universities (multiculturalism and critical race studies are some of the others). For Kimball, the emergence of cultural studies in general is nothing short of a

> **❝ A kind of intellectual freak show. ❞**
> Roger Kimball, "'Diversity', 'Cultural Studies' & Other Mistakes"

"politically charged intellectual virus, which at many institutions has transformed the teaching of the humanities into a kind of intellectual freak show."[1]

Other critics who have engaged with *Epistemology of The Closet* on more substantive intellectual grounds include the geographer, Michael Brown, the LGBT cultural studies researcher, David Van Leer, and the literary scholar, Terry Castle. Both Brown and Van Leer take issue with the particular way in which Sedgwick deploys the concept of the closet.[2] The relentless textuality of Sedgwick's analysis, they argue, obscures its material and spatial realities. However, Van Leer takes his critique a step further, insisting that by overlooking the practical historical function of the closet, Sedgwick reproduces the very homophobia she aims to dismantle. Castle's criticisms meanwhile represent a lesbian counterpoint to Sedgwick's largely male-centered analysis.[3] Castle associates Sedgwick's work with the tendency of cultural studies to lump gay men and women together, effectively erasing lesbian experience under the universalizing category "queer."

Responses

Among the most notable exchanges between Sedgwick and one of her critics is her dialogue with David Van Leer. In 1989 Van Leer published an article in the influential journal *Critical Inquiry,* entitled "The Beast of the Closet: Homosociality and the Pathology of Manhood," which took aim at Sedgwick's 1985 book *Between Men.* Van Leer argues that by persistently using homosexuality to frame "larger" questions of sexual politics, *Between Men* plays fast and loose with the actual experience of gay men. As well, he accuses Sedgwick of reproducing negative stereotypes of gay men (as effeminate, for example) in her writing. For Van Leer, Sedgwick ends up reinforcing the homophobic thematics that she purports to uncover.[4]

That same year Sedgwick penned a response to Van Leer in the same publication called "Tide and Trust."[5] Here Sedgwick characterizes Van Leer's essay as essentially a misreading of her work; however, this is not to say that she does not take Van Leer's critique seriously. In particular, the accusation of homophobia levelled at her by Van Leer was not something she could simply dismiss outright. As Jason Edwards notes, Sedgwick "took seriously the idea that there was nobody who was not homophobic, racist, or sexist."[6] If, as Sedgwick argues so eruditely in *Epistemology of The Closet,* the distinction of homo/heterosexuality, and thus homophobia, informs the very formation of modern categories of knowledge, then "to exist as a person and to construct an argument … almost inescapably implicated an individual in some form of homophobia."[7] Sedgwick's "Tide and Trade" prompted a further rebuttal from Van Leer, "Trust and Trade: A Response to Sedgwick" (also in 1989).[8] And in his 1995 monograph, *The Queering of America,* Van Leer refocused his critique on both *Between Men* and *Epistemology of The Closet,* arguing that by emphasizing the closet as a category of ontology rather than history, "Sedgwick minimizes the practical reasons for being in the closet."[9] Although Van Leer's criticisms were initially penned, not in response to *Epistemology of The Closet,* but to Sedgwick's preceding book, it is noteworthy that she would have been engaged in this exchange— rejecting claims of homophobia, accounting for her interest in gay men (incongruous to some given her own heterosexual attachments), and recapitulating her arguments—in the immediate lead up to the publication of *Epistemology of The Closet* in 1990.

Conflict and Consensus

Although the depth of her exchange with Van Leer suggests that Sedgwick took seriously substantive critiques of her work, it would be wrong to suggest that they alone prompted any fundamental modification to her philosophy. With respect to the broader institutional criticism about the legitimacy of cultural studies, Sedgwick was undeterred. She continued to champion experimental forms of inquiry in cultural studies throughout her career. This is not to say, however, that she defended the discipline as something self-evident and fixed. Sedgwick's alliance was not with any field or discipline, but with the belief that intellectual work begins where the boundaries of disciplinary knowledge begin to waver. While debates about the legitimacy of fields like queer studies, gender and sexuality studies, and critical race studies endure, cultural studies has undeniably become an influential fixture in the academy. Yet, every once in while a story emerges ridiculing cultural studies based on a statement or research question taken out of context that putatively shows just how "wacky" and/or politicized universities have become. Criticisms like Kimball's about the politicization of the humanities tend to reveal what does and *does not* counts as political in the first place. To put this another way, while queer and feminist scholars may seem to be more political in their work than their traditionalist counterparts, the manner in which certain methods, texts, and preoccupation come to be viewed as politically-neutral is itself deeply political. Likewise, those who see lesbian and gay studies, Queer Theory, and feminism as making everything about sex and gender, fail to see the ways in which ideas about sex and gender lies at the heart of the traditional Western canon they seek to preserve.

NOTES

1   Roger Kimball, "'Diversity', 'Cultural Studies' & Other Mistakes," *The New Criterion* 14, no. 9 (1996): 4–9.

2   See: Michael Brown, *Closet Space: Geographies of the Metaphor from the Body to the Globe* (London: Routledge, 2000); and David Van Leer, "The Beast of the Closet: Homosociality and the Pathology of Manhood," *Critical Inquiry* 15, no.3 (1989): 587–605.

3   Terry Castle, *The Apparitional Lesbian: Female Homosexuality and Modern Culture* (New York: Columbia University Press, 1993). See also: Blakey Vermeule, "Is There a Sedgwick School for Girls?," *Qui Parle* 5, no. 1 (1991): 53–72.

4   David Van Leer, "The Beast of the Closet: Homosociality and the Pathology of Manhood," *Critical Inquiry* 15, no.3 (1989): 587–605.

5   Eve Kosofsky Sedgwick, "Tide and Trust," *Critical Inquiry* 15, no. 4 (1989): 745–57.

6   Jason Edwards, *Eve Kosofsky Sedgwick* (London: Routledge, 2009), 138.

7   Edwards, *Eve Kosofsky Sedgwick*, 138.

8   David Van Leer, "Trust and Trade," *Critical Inquiry* 15, no. 4 (1989): 758–63.

9   David Van Leer, *The Queening of America: Gay Culture in Straight Society* (New York: Routledge, 1995), 111.

THE EVOLVING DEBATE

KEY POINTS

- Affect theory and performance studies* are among the fields of inquiry which have roots in Sedgwick's work.

- Along with Judith Butler, Sedgwick is seen as a foundational figure of Queer Theory as a school of thought.

- Queer theory as a field continues to evolve in dynamic ways today.

Uses and Problems

Much contemporary work in cultural studies and critical theory can be traced back to *Epistemology of the Closet* and its pivotal role in helping to establish Queer Theory. Perhaps two of the most dynamic areas of research associated with Sedgwick's work are affect theory and performance studies. In later texts such as *Touching Feeling,* we see how Sedgwick's groundbreaking work in Queer Theory developed into a deep interest in questions of feeling, pleasure, and expression. This theoretical trajectory in Sedgwick's work coincides with what has been called the affective turn in the humanities more broadly. Affect theory is concerned with the dimension of feelings and intensities that do not rise to the level of what can be put into words or experienced as conscious cognition. Like other prominent affect theorist such as Laurent Berlant, Sara Ahmed, and José Esteban Muñoz, Sedgwick saw affect as central to thinking through the embodied experience of social, psychic, and political life.

Much of Sedgwick's thinking on affect in *Touching Feeling* stems from a the idea of performance. As an academic field, performance

> ❝ Queer theory's intellectual concerns have given rise to newer kinds of work, and are continued under other rubrics. ❞
>
> Michael Warner, "Queer and Then?"

studies is concerned not only with theatrical events, but also "performativity" in a much broader sense. Influenced heavily by the work of J. L. Austin, Sedgwick's exploration of performativity in *Touching Feeling* expands upon Austin's observations about the ways in which speech *acts* in the world. Certain utterances such as "I promise," or, most famously, the "I do" of marriage, make saying and doing one in the same. "Austinian performativity," Sedgwick writes, "is about how language constructs or affects reality rather than merely describing it."[1] Sedgwick's writings on affect and performativity reflect a deep-seated interest in the intertwined nature of language, literature, intimacy, and, indeed, politics. Ongoing work in affect and performativity reflect the multiple intellectual tributaries that have—at least in part—emerged from Sedgwick's groundbreaking work in *Epistemology of The Closet*.

Schools of Thought

Along with Judith Butler, Sedgwick is often referred to as the founder of Queer Theory. As a school of thought, Queer Theory emphasizes the ways sexuality is socially constructed. It can be contrasted with gay and lesbian studies, which emphasizes the recovery of the concealed and repressed culture and history of specifically gay and lesbian actors. Queer Theory, by contrast, does not take gay and lesbian as self-evident categories, and thus does not limit its analysis to the works and experience of homosexual people, *per se*. Instead, it seeks to explore the ways in which different categories of sexual life such as gay/straight and normal/perverse are mutually constituted through relations of power and discourse. Additionally, it explores the ways sexuality produces and is produced by other, seemingly unrelated, ideas about identity, desire, bodies, and politics. Given the keenly interdisciplinary nature of the Queer Theory she helped to pioneer, the parameters of Sedgwick's intellectual influence are difficult to map. Needless to say, Queer Theory continues to be an influential force in the humanities and social sciences. Yet, as is described in the previous section, this is not Sedgwick's only legacy. Related schools of thought such as Affect Theory and performance studies also bear the stamp of Sedgwick's thinking.

In Current Scholarship

Among those scholars not already mentioned who continue to develop Sedgwick's ideas and who have, in some sense, inherited her legacy include: Heather Love, whose work looks at what lies behind gay and lesbian people's trek into mainstream culture; Elizabeth Freeman, whose work explores the queerness of time and the temporalities of queerness; and Mel Y. Chen, whose work charts new paths in thinking about the relationship between the categories of animate and inanimate matter. These prominent American scholars reflect some of the different avenues of inquiry that have built upon Sedgwick's foundational work in theorizing queerness. As these and other scholars continue to push Queer Theory in new and diverse directions, we see how *Epistemology of The Closet* and Sedgwick's oeuvre more broadly remains a rich resource for new avenues of thought not yet defined in disciplinary terms. In a 2012 essay on the current state of Queer Theory, Michael Warner writes that "Queer Theory's intellectual concerns have given rise to newer kinds of work, and are continued under other rubrics."[2] Thus, while prominent scholars in and around the overlapping arenas of Queer Theory, Affect Theory, and performativity can be seen as the torch bearers of Sedgwick's work, perhaps her greatest legacy is a model for ways of thinking and reading that work through and past the institutional framings of scholarship, including those of Queer Theory itself.

NOTES

1   Eve Kosofsky Sedgwick, *Touching Feeling: Affect, Pedagogy, Performativity* (Durham: Duke UP, 2003), 5.

2   Michael Warner, "Queer and Then?" *The Chronicle of Higher Education Review*, January 1, 2012, accessed June 1, 2013, http://chronicle.com/article/QueerThen-/130161.

MODULE 11
IMPACT AND INFLUENCE TODAY

KEY POINTS

- Sedgwick's legacy is not only as a groundbreaking scholar, but also as an admired teacher, artist, activist, colleague, and creative interlocutor.

- Queer Theory continuously questions and challenges the assumptions behind what counts as a legitimate object and method of study.

- If Sedgwick were alive, she would very likely be engaged in challenging the prevalent conservative critique of the university today.

Position

Sedgwick's untimely death in 2009 precipitated a public reflection by many on the enduring influence of her life and work. There is no doubt that Sedgwick's status, as one of the founders of Queer Theory, means she will continue to be a prominent figure in and around the fields of critical theory and cultural studies. But it is also worth noting that the recognition of Sedgwick's legacy following her death often focused on her work as teacher, mentor, colleague, and creative interlocutor. In her brief tribute to Sedgwick, Lauren Berlant—now one of the leading figures of queer and affect theories—wrote that Sedgwick's "position was fundamentally as a teacher."[1] Sedgwick had the capacity, Berlant writes, to "create a scene of genuinely transformative pedagogy." The warm, if also sometimes critical, assessment of Sedgwick's life work reminds us of something she herself often observed—that philosophical work does not happen in a

❝ Sedgwick's career seems to provide not only a paradigm of the evolution of contemporary literary theory, but also of a contemporary feminist intellectual. **❞**
Elaine Showalter, "Vibrating to the Chord of Queer"

vacuum, nor should it, and that interactions, intimacies, and affect are inseparable from the work of critique.

There are several reasons for the enduring significance of *Epistemology of the Closet* today. For one, *Epistemology of The Closet* continues to serve as a model for the difficult task of broaching rigorous literary analysis and questions of politics, identity, and embodied experience. More specifically, the volume is indispensable as an application and elaboration of Foucault's work on the mutually constituting categories of discourse, sexuality, and power. Finally, as an experiment in testing the boundaries of feminism and literary criticism, *Epistemology of The Closet* remains a powerful testament to the importance of challenging traditional and hegemonic modes of disciplinary research and pedagogy in the academy.

Interaction

One of the main ways Queer Theory squares off against its opponents is by perpetually challenging the assumptions of what counts as legitimate in the realms of politics and academia. Like the famous feminist maxim, "the personal is political," Queer Theory is often preoccupied with disrupting categorical distinctions—such as the personal *and* political. Critics of Queer Theory tend to characterize it as either theoretically verbose and self-serving, or as a troubling politicization of humanist scholarship. Sedgwick may not necessarily have disagreed with these characterizations. Although Sedgwick could hardly have aimed at being difficult for difficulty's sake, she firmly believed in the necessity of confronting the complexity of texts and language. Sedgwick never shied away from politicizing the academy because she never saw the university as anything other than a political entity.

By the early 1990s, Sedgwick had become a symbol to many of the wanton radicalization of the humanities. One of Sedgwick's title's—originally the name of a Modern Languages Association conference presentation—drew particular ire. This was "Jane Austen and the Masturbating Girl," which for many journalists and academics alike epitomized the corruption of American universities through the institutionalization of cultural studies. In a subsequent discussion of this criticism, Sedgwick notes the personal nature of the attacks she received. "The attacks on me personally," she writes, "were based on such scummy evidential procedures that the most thin-skinned of scholars—so long as their livelihood was secure— could hardly have taken them to heart."[2] The attacks on "Jane Austen and the Masturbating Girl," came not so much from a moral condemnation of masturbation itself, as from the fear that academics were willfully engaging in a kind of "mental masturbation." Sedgwick relates the distaste some felt for the title of her Jane Austen piece with the perpetual fear academics face of being seen as engaged in frivolous work. What for Sedgwick was one of Queer Theory's strengths—its readiness to explore those things that might seem "merely" personal—was for many an indication of a willful embrace of frivolousness in the academy.

The Continuing Debate

Although criticism that rejects Queer Theory and cultural studies more broadly may not be as prominent as it once was inside universities, it continues to fuel the arguably growing perception that education and research in the humanities is increasingly irrelevant. In *Tenured Radicals*, Roger Kimball argues that the institutional establishment of fields such as women's studies, black studies, gay studies, as well as the new interpretive role semiotics, deconstruction, and poststructuralism play, are nothing short of "ideologically motivated assaults on the intellectual and moral substance of our culture."[3] Kimball may not be a popular figure on course curriculum today, but his reactionary perspective is consistent with contemporary attacks on the university by conservatives. Kimball saw the rise of cultural studies as "a concerted effort to attack the very foundations of the society that guarantees the independence of cultural and artistic life."[4] And it is certainly possible to see this criticism as part of the broader, ongoing critique of higher education, one that argues that the university has become a bastion for leftist ideologues intent on squashing free speech in blind pursuit of "safe spaces" and a narrow identity-based or "snowflake" political revolution.

NOTES

1   Lauren Berlant, "Eve Sedgwick, Once More," *Critical Inquiry* 35 (2009): 1089–91. See also: Lauren Berlant, "After Eve, In Honor of Eve Kosofsky Sedgwick," Reseach blog, *Supervalent Thought* (blog), March 18, 2010, http://supervalentthought.com/2010/03/18/after-eve-in-honor-of-eve-kosofsky-sedgwick/.

2   Eve Kosofsky Sedgwick, *Tendencies* (Durham: Routledge, 1994),16.

3   Roger Kimball, *Tenured Radicals: How Politics Has Corrupted Our Higher Education* (New York: Harper & Row, 1990), 10-11.

4   Kimball, *Tenured Radicals*, 14.

WHERE NEXT?

KEY POINTS

- Sedgwick remains not simply an important historical proponent of Queer Theory, but also an enduring influence in shaping its future.

- There is significant real-world application for Sedgwick's ideas.

- Sedgwick has helped to shape how a generation of scholars think about the relationship between identity, desire, and power.

Potential

In *Epistemology of the Closet,* Sedgwick shows how the gay closet operates as a site of knowledge, implicating homosexuals and heterosexuals alike. No doubt much has changed with respect to the closet since the early 1990s. Western cultures are more tolerant of homosexuality, and gay men and women generally feel freer to disclose their homosexuality, yet sexuality more broadly remains something framed largely in terms of hiddenness and exposure. Even if we accept that people in Western liberal societies generally feel freer to come out of the closet than they did twenty-five years ago, the question of what any particular person is "into" sexually is often subject to the same logic of secrecy and revelation. It is impossible to see any given person's sexuality as either fully expressed or repressed. In this sense, Sedgwick's discussion of the closet remains highly relevant to critical discourses of sexuality. The enduring value of *Epistemology of The Closet,* however, does not rest in what it reveals of sexuality alone. Another enduring aspect of the text is the methodological approach it helped to develop

> **❝** So many people of varying sexual practices, too, enjoy incorrigibly absorbing imaginative, artistic, intellectual, and affective lives that have been richly nourished by queer energies—and that are savagely diminished when the queerness of those energies is traded or disavowed. **❞**
>
> Eve Kosofsky Sedgwick, *Tendencies*

for analyzing social and cultural formations more broadly. In particular, *Epistemology of The Closet* helped to establish Queer Theory's central focus on deconstructing binary categories of identity, be they explicitly sexual or not.

Firmly planted as one of the foundational texts of the still-burgeoning fields of queer studies, affect theory, and performance studies, *Epistemology of The Closet* will no doubt continue to be read, debated, and reinterpreted by students and scholars for decades to come. In recent years the future of Queer Theory—the school of thought established in the 1990s and that *Epistemology of The Closet* helped to pioneer—has been the subject of intense debate among feminists and scholars of lesbian and gay studies, and gender and sexuality studies. Many have sought to demarcate a "post-queer" era, imagining its "afterlives," questioning its contemporary utility, and diagnosing its failures. Where such debates do take place, they are rarely without reference to *Epistemology of The Closet*. This is a testament to the fact that Sedgwick remains, not simply an important historical figure in the story of Queer Theory, but also an enduring influence in shaping its future. As a theory that advocates for the questioning of the perceived and enforced categories by which we understand ourselves and the world, the direction of Queer Theory is necessarily impossible to predict.

Future Directions

Prominent figures in the field of gender and sexuality studies continue to put the notion "queer" in conversation with new topics of study. In *Time Binds: Queer Temporalities, Queer Histories,* Elizabeth Freeman, for example, draws on Sedgwick's discussion of gay children to develop her conceptualizations of queer time. Other research such as Jasbir Puar's work on the racialized body (politic) of the "war on terror," and Scott Morgensen's work on "settler homonationalism" have explored the limits and violence of queer identity (and Queer Theory) in discussions of colonialism, nationalism, and capitalism. Evidence of the durability of Queer Theory is also evidenced by the new book series, *Theory Q,* edited by two of the field's most prominent figures, Lauren Berlant and Lee Edelman. *Theory Q* is a reissue of the influential series, *Series Q,* edited by Sedgwick and others.

In speaking of the future direction of *Epistemology of The Closet,* it is worth providing a concrete illustration of its potential application in examining contemporary phenomena. It would not be difficult, for example, to show how Sedgwick's core argument about the incongruities between the minoritizing and universalizing logics of the closet could be applied to the current opioid crisis taking place in North America. Imagine this: the mother and father of a "regular" middle-class family—a white family—sharing their grief about the overdose death of their son or daughter to a mainstream news organization in hopes that by telling their story they might help save even just one life. The poignancy of this kind of scenario, which has characterized recent media coverage of the overdose crisis, seems to involve two contradictory messages, "this can happen to anyone," and "this isn't supposed to happen to *us.*" In other words, it involves both the universalizing logic of "the dangers of drugs are universal," and "it's not for normal people to experience the dangers of drugs." Furthermore, by revealing the illicit activities of their otherwise "normal" son or daughter, the parents *perform* secrecy even while they obscure the known truth that drugs have long been a part of white middle-class life. These contradictions and switchbacks of revelation and concealment are what Sedgwick calls the spectacle of the closet. This familiar scenario is, to quote Sedgwick, "bayonetted through and through, from both sides, by the vectors of a disclosure at once compulsory and forbidden."[1] Commentators have noted the discrepancy between the drug wars of the 1980s, in which drug use and overdose was associated with "gangs" and "ghettos," and the current discourse around the opioid crisis, which is framed as an emergency for "ordinary" Americans. No doubt there is more that could be explored in terms of the ways the spectacle of the closet, as described here, operates in ways that are class and race specific. As this example suggests, the spectacle of the closet is hardly limited to the issue or representation of homosexuality *per se*.

Summary

In *Regarding Sedgwick,* a 2002 collection dedicated to Sedgwick's work, Stephen Barber and David Clark argue that Sedgwick changed for a generation of scholars and activists "how we think about the nexus of identity, desires, bodies, prohibition, discourses, and the play of power."[2] After Sedgwick, homosexuality can no longer be seen as an isolated issue or experience. What *Epistemology of Closet* shows is that the taxonomic distinction between homo- and heterosexual is not merely the product of modern society; rather it informs and configures virtually all aspects of modern Western culture.[3] Thus, Epistemology of The Closet makes a radical case for developing critical methods that use homosexuality or queerness as a frame for other aspects of life and politics that seemingly have little to do with sex, no less gay sex. But as much as Sedgwick's third and best-known book should be recognized as a radical intervention in feminist and sexuality studies, it must also be noted for its layered and often subtle insights on the complex relations between the textuality of desire and the intimacies of texts. Like all of Sedgwick's writing, *Epistemology of The Closet* is an intricate and textured work that has the capacity to reveal new insights with every reading.

NOTES

1   Eve Kosofsky Sedgwick, *Epistemology of the Closet* (Berkeley: University of California Press, 1990), 70.

2   Stephen M. Barber and David L. Clark, eds., *Regarding Sedgwick: Essays on Queer Culture and Critical Theory* (London: Routledge, 2002), 3.

3   Sedgwick, 1.

GLOSSARY

GLOSSARY OF TERMS

Affect Theory: the study of lived experiences that are not conscious or verbal.

Canon: is the collection of authors and texts that are accepted among scholars as the most significant to the culture and thus most worthy of study.

Civil Rights Movement: a struggle for social justice that took place mainly during the 1950s and '60s for blacks to gain equal rights under the law in the United States.

Constructionism: a theoretical perspective that emphasizes the way experience is produced through discursive meaning. Constructionism is contrasted with theories that appeal to universal and biological explanations of why things are the way they are.

Cultural Studies: a disciplinary field that focuses on the way the world in constructed through notions of difference and identity, and through relations of power, knowledge, affect, desire, capital and material culture.

Culture wars: often characterized as a contest between those seeking to preserve the traditional English canon (and attendant literary methods of criticism) and those who sought to "democratize" the kinds of texts and cultural objects that were recognized as legitimate objects of study. In the context of debates in higher education during the 1980s, the "culture wars" describes a period of contention and refocusing in the Humanities that brought about new research and teaching on ethnic, women's, and lesbian and gay studies.

Discourse: refers to the system of symbols and categories that allows state and cultural institutions to operate, and thus to exert power.

Deconstruction (or deconstructionism): a method of textual analysis where linguistic meaning is understood as inherently unstable and shifting, and where readers, rather than authors, determine its tentative meanings. Its earliest development is credited to the French philosopher Jacques Derrida.

Epistemology: the study of knowledge, its sources, and statuses.

Feminism: a school of thought that explores the power relations between the sexes and brings the oppression and experiences of women into view.

Gay Rights Movement: a social and political movement dated, in the Anglo-American context, to the late 1960s, which calls for the recognition and equal protection of gays and lesbians under the law. Gay Rights is sometimes used interchangeably with Gay Liberation, but the latter is more revolutionary and radical than the former, questioning the structures of power rather than simply seeking inclusion within them.

Lesbian and Gay Studies: an academic field that emerged in the 1970s and considers the often suppressed historical and cultural significance of homosexual people and their work. It can be distinguished from Queer Theory in that the latter emphasizes the culturally constructed and unstable nature of identities such as lesbian and gay.

Marxism: a school of the thought based on the work of the German economic philosopher and historian, Karl Marx (1818-1883).

Marxism emphasizes capitalism as a societal, as well as economic, system whereby the ruling class derives exponential ideological power and material wealth by exploiting the basic needs of the working majority.

McCarthyism: a vociferous and derisive campaign against alleged communists in the United States led by senator Joseph McCarthy in the early 1950s.

Minoritizing (view of homosexuality): a key neologism in Sedgwick's *Epistemology of the Closet*. Contrasted with the universalizing view of homosexuality, the minoritizing view is defined as seeing homo/heterosexual definition as an issue of active importance primarily for a small, distinct, relatively fixed homosexual minority.

Performance Studies: is an interdisciplinary field of study that uses performance as a frame for analyzing the world. It draws from, but is not limited in scope to, the formal contexts of stage performance, and is closely associated with the concept of performativity as developed by J. L. Austin, Judith Butler, and others.

Performativity: is a concept associated with "performative" utterances or statements that bring into being that which it refers to. The speech act "I sentence you ..." in the court of law exemplifies this concept. The concept is associated with J. L. Austin and Judith Butler who have shown the complex effects of performativity in various social and cultural contexts.

Positivist (or positivism): a philosophical doctrine that collapses science and reality together, and holds that nonscientific claims, such as those of myth, religion, and metaphysics are not genuine forms of knowledge.

Postmodernism: an academic mode of inquiry, but also a characterization of a much broader shift in modernity, denoting an ambivalence towards master narratives, and a foregrounding of irony, pastiche, genre blurring, and "meta" discourses.

Poststructuralism: an intellectual reaction to structuralism, it can be broadly defined as an approach to philosophy and other disciplines that seeks complexity in the contingency of language and holds that it is impossible to permanently fix as an object of study the structures that constitute human experience. It is associated with the late twentieth century French philosophers Jacques Derrida, Michel Foucault, and Gilles Deleuze.

Psychoanalysis: a body of thought and therapeutic practice developed from the writings of Sigmund Freud (1856–1939) and centered in large part on the notion of the unconscious.

Queerness: During the 1990's, members of the LGBT community and political organizations such as ACT-UP and Queer Nation assumed the terms "queer" and "queerness" as a moniker of their sexual identity. These individuals and groups sought to re-signify the injurious meanings of the word, recuperating its provocative edge as an affirmative expression of anti-assimilationist politics. The term thus involves a greater sense of political provocation and cultural subversion than "homosexual" or "gay."

Queer Theory: is an interdisciplinary field that explores the cultural construction of sexual identities including their plurality and ambivalence. It challenges received notions about the biological, empirical, and cultural bases of gender and sexuality. Unlike lesbian and gay identity politics, it does not regard acceptance into mainstream society as its objective, but rather seeks the transformation of the heterosexual basis of society itself.

Second Wave (Feminism): refers to a period of feminist activity and thought from roughly the mid-1960s to the early '70s. Whereas First Wave Feminism refers mainly to the Women's Suffrage Movement, the Second Wave sought greater equality for women across the board in areas such as education, the workplace, and the home. Some more recent transformations of feminism have been described as a "Third Wave." Third Wave feminists often criticize Second Wave feminism for its emphasis on the experience of liberal white woman, and for its lack of attention to the differences among women such as race, class, nationality, education, and religion.

Semiotics: the study of signs and symbols and their uses and interpretations.

Stonewall: refers the to the events of June 27, 1969, in which lesbians, gay men, and cross-dressed men and women fought back against legalized police harassment and violence. Centered at the Stonewall Inn in Greenwich Village, New York City, direct actions took place for five days demanding an end to the systemic targeting of gay and trans people, events which are today widely cited as the beginning of Gay Liberation and the Gay Rights Movements.

Universalizing (view of homosexuality): contrasted with what Sedgwick calls the minoritizing view, the universalizing view of homosexuality holds that homosexuality is an issue of continuing, determinative importance in the lives of people across the spectrum of sexualities.

PEOPLE MENTIONED IN THE TEXT

J. L. Austin (1911–60) was a British philosopher of language. His work has been an important influence for a wide variety of contemporary scholarship operating under the banner of performance studies.

Lauren Berlant (b. 1957) is a prominent American queer theorist focusing on questions of intimacy and citizenship, as well as series editor of *Theory Q* (Duke University Press).

Judith Butler (b. 1956) is Professor of Rhetoric and Comparative Literature at the University California, Berkeley. She is well known, along with Eve Kosofsky Sedgwick, as one of the founders of Queer Theory, this following the 1990 publication of her seminal text, *Gender Trouble: Feminism and the Subversion of Identity* (London: Routledge, 1990).

Jason Edwards (b. unknown) is Professor of the History of Art History at the University of York. He is a leading figure in the study of Eve Kosofsky Sedgwick's critical and artistic work.

Michel Foucault (1926–84) was a major figure in French philosophy who wrote a number of extremely influential books about the interrelated functions of knowledge and power. He is a key figure in Queer Theory and Sexuality Studies among numerous other fields.

Lady Gaga (b. 1986) is an American pop singer, song writer, actress, and advocate for a number of causes. She's known for her extravagant fashion and as an icon in the gay community.

Henry James (1843–1916) was a prolific American-born novelist and literary critic. Much of his life was spent in England and Europe, and his writing often considers the distinctions between American and European class mores and the figure of the American abroad.

Roger Kimball (b. 1953) is an American art critic, social commentator, and editor and publisher of the conservative literary journal *The New Criterion*. He is the author of many books including *Tenured Radicals: How Politics Has Corrupted Our Higher Education,* a polemic against what he describes an ideological assault on Western civilization lead by radical leftist professors in elite humanities departments across the United States.

Herman Melville (1819–91) was an American novelist. He is best known as the author of the novel *Moby-Dick* (1951), based in part on his own experience as a whaler and seaman. In *Epistemology of the Closet,* Sedgwick looks at an earlier novella by Melville, *Billy Budd* (first published posthumously in 1924).

Friedrich Wilhelm Nietzsche (1844–1890) was a German philosopher and is considered by many to be one of the most important thinkers of modern times. His famous expression, "God is dead" from his 1882 collection, *The Gay Science,* is among the most cited phrases of modern philosophy.

Ann Pellegrini (b. 1964) is Professor of Performance Studies at the Tisch School of the Arts and of Social and Cultural Analysis in the Faculty of Arts and Sciences, New York University.

Marcel Proust (1871–1922) was a French novelist, essayist, and critic. He is best known for his monumental novel, *In Search of Lost*

Time (english trans.) Sedgwick examines this novel in *Epistemology of the Closet*—in particular the section called "Sodom and Gomorrah."

Ronald Reagan (1911-2004) was an American Republican statesman and the 40th president of the United States (1981-89). A Hollywood actor before entering politics, his presidency saw the launch of the Strategic Defence Initiative, cuts in taxes and social services, as well as soaring national debt.

Matthew Shepard (1976-1998) was a university student in Laramie, WY, when he was the victim of a brutal assault and murder. He was targeted in part because he was gay. The crime brought national attention to the issue of violence against gays and mobilized calls for greater hate-crime legislation.

David Van Leer (1949–2013) was an American scholar of US culture and history, often working within lesbian and gay studies. From 1986 he was Professor of English at the University of California Davis.

Michael Warner (b. 1958) is an American literary critic and social theorist. Like Eve Kosofsky Sedgwick, he is considered a central figure in the field of Queer Theory.

Oscar Wilde (1854–1900) was an Irish dramatist and famous wit. Much of his notoriety came with the production of a number of successful plays, including *The Importance of Being Earnest* (1895), which display his shrewd observation of upper-middle-class English manners, as well as his controversial views about art. In 1895 Wilde was convicted and imprisoned for homosexual offences. In *Epistemology of the Closet,* Sedgwick looks at *The Picture of Dorian Gray,* Wilde's only novel (first published in 1890).

WORKS CITED

WORKS CITED

Barber, Stephen M., and David L. Clark, eds. *Regarding Sedgwick: Essays on Queer Culture and Critical Theory*. London: Routledge, 2002.

Berlant, Lauren. "After Eve, In Honor of Eve Kosofsky Sedgwick." Reseach blog. *Supervalent Thought* (blog), March 18, 2010. http://supervalentthought.com/2010/03/18/after-eve-in-honor-of-eve-kosofsky-sedgwick/.

"Eve Sedgwick, Once More." *Critical Inquiry* 35 (2009): 1089–91.

Brown, Michael. *Closet Space: Geographies of the Metaphor from the Body to the Globe*. London: Routledge, 2000.

Butler, Judith. *Gender Trouble: Feminism and the Subversion of Identity*. London: Routledge, 2006.

Castle, Terry. *The Apparitional Lesbian: Female Homosexulality and Modern Culture*. New York: Routledge, 1993.

Edwards, Jason. *Eve Kosofsky Sedgwick*. London: Routledge, 2009.

Foucault, Michel. *The History of Sexuality, Vol. 1: An Introduction*. Translated by Robert Hurley. New York: Vintage, 1978.

Freeman, Elizabeth. *Time Binds: Queer Temporalities, Queer Histories*. Durham NC: Duke University Press, 2010.

Kimball, Roger. "'Diversity,' 'Cultural Studies' & Other Mistakes." *The New Criterion*, May 1996.

Tenured Radicals: How Politics Has Corrupted Our Higher Education. New York: Harper & Row, 1990.

Morgensen, Scott Lauria. "Settler Homonationalism: Theorizing Settler Colonialism within Queer Modernities." *GLQ: A Journal of Lesbian and Gay Studies* 16, no. 1–2 (2010): 105–31.

Pellegrini, Ann. "Eve Kosofsky Sedgwick." *The Chronicle of Higher Education*, May 8, 2009. https://www.chronicle.com/article/Eve-Kosofsky-Sedgwick/15045.

Phillips, Sarah. "Eve Kosofsky Sedgwick." *The Guardian*, May 12, 2009, sec.

Books.

Puar, Jasbir K. *Terrorist Assemblages: Homonationalism in Queer Times*. Durham: Duke University Press, 2007.

Sedgwick, Eve Kosofsky. *A Dialogue on Love*. Boston: Beacon Press, 2000.

Between Men: English Literature and Male Homosocial Desire. New York: Columbia University Press, 1985.

Epistemology of the Closet. Berkeley: University of California Press, 1990.

"Sedgwick Sense and Sensibility: An Interview with Eve Kosofsky Sedgwick." Interview by Mark Kerr and Kristin O'Rourke, c 1995. http://nideffer.net/proj/Tvc/interviews/20.Tvc.v9.intrvws.Sedg.html.

Tendencies. Durham: Routledge, 1994.

"Tide and Trust." *Critical Inquiry* 15, no. 4 (1989): 745–57.

Touching Feeling: Affect, Pedagogy, Performativity. Durham: Duke UP, 2003.

Showalter, Elaine. "Vibrating to the Chord of Queer." *London Review of Books* 25, no. 5 (March 6, 2003): 10–11.

Smith, Dinitia. "'Queer Theory' Is Entering the Literary Mainstream." *The New York Times*, January 17, 1998, sec. Books. https://www.nytimes.com/1998/01/17/books/queer-theory-is-entering-the-literary-mainstream.html.

Van Leer, David. "The Beast of the Closet: Homosociality and the Pathology of Manhood." *Critical Inquiry* 15, no. 3 (1989): 587–605.

The Queening of America: Gay Culture in Straight Society. New York: Routledge, 1995.

"Trust and Trade." *Critical Inquiry* 15, no. 4 (1989): 745–57.

Vermeule, Blakey. "Is There a Sedgwick School for Girls?" *Qui Parle* 5, no. 1 (1991): 53–72.

THE MACAT LIBRARY
BY DISCIPLINE

AFRICANA STUDIES

Chinua Achebe's *An Image of Africa: Racism in Conrad's Heart of Darkness*
W. E. B. Du Bois's *The Souls of Black Folk*
Zora Neale Huston's *Characteristics of Negro Expression*
Martin Luther King Jr's *Why We Can't Wait*
Toni Morrison's *Playing in the Dark: Whiteness in the American Literary Imagination*

ANTHROPOLOGY

Arjun Appadurai's *Modernity at Large: Cultural Dimensions of Globalisation*
Philippe Ariès's *Centuries of Childhood*
Franz Boas's *Race, Language and Culture*
Kim Chan & Renée Mauborgne's *Blue Ocean Strategy*
Jared Diamond's *Guns, Germs & Steel: the Fate of Human Societies*
Jared Diamond's *Collapse: How Societies Choose to Fail or Survive*
E. E. Evans-Pritchard's *Witchcraft, Oracles and Magic Among the Azande*
James Ferguson's *The Anti-Politics Machine*
Clifford Geertz's *The Interpretation of Cultures*
David Graeber's *Debt: the First 5000 Years*
Karen Ho's *Liquidated: An Ethnography of Wall Street*
Geert Hofstede's *Culture's Consequences: Comparing Values, Behaviors, Institutes and Organizations across Nations*
Claude Lévi-Strauss's *Structural Anthropology*
Jay Macleod's *Ain't No Makin' It: Aspirations and Attainment in a Low-Income Neighborhood*
Saba Mahmood's *The Politics of Piety: The Islamic Revival and the Feminist Subjec*t
Marcel Mauss's *The Gift*

BUSINESS

Jean Lave & Etienne Wenger's *Situated Learning*
Theodore Levitt's *Marketing Myopia*
Burton G. Malkiel's *A Random Walk Down Wall Street*
Douglas McGregor's *The Human Side of Enterprise*
Michael Porter's *Competitive Strategy: Creating and Sustaining Superior Performance*
John Kotter's *Leading Change*
C. K. Prahalad & Gary Hamel's *The Core Competence of the Corporation*

CRIMINOLOGY

Michelle Alexander's *The New Jim Crow: Mass Incarceration in the Age of Colorblindness*
Michael R. Gottfredson & Travis Hirschi's *A General Theory of Crime*
Richard Herrnstein & Charles A. Murray's *The Bell Curve: Intelligence and Class Structure in American Life*
Elizabeth Loftus's *Eyewitness Testimony*
Jay Macleod's *Ain't No Makin' It: Aspirations and Attainment in a Low-Income Neighborhood*
Philip Zimbardo's *The Lucifer Effect*

ECONOMICS

Janet Abu-Lughod's *Before European Hegemony*
Ha-Joon Chang's *Kicking Away the Ladder*
David Brion Davis's *The Problem of Slavery in the Age of Revolution*
Milton Friedman's *The Role of Monetary Policy*
Milton Friedman's *Capitalism and Freedom*
David Graeber's *Debt: the First 5000 Years*
Friedrich Hayek's *The Road to Serfdom*
Karen Ho's *Liquidated: An Ethnography of Wall Street*

The Macat Library By Discipline

John Maynard Keynes's *The General Theory of Employment, Interest and Money*
Charles P. Kindleberger's *Manias, Panics and Crashes*
Robert Lucas's *Why Doesn't Capital Flow from Rich to Poor Countries?*
Burton G. Malkiel's *A Random Walk Down Wall Street*
Thomas Robert Malthus's *An Essay on the Principle of Population*
Karl Marx's *Capital*
Thomas Piketty's *Capital in the Twenty-First Century*
Amartya Sen's *Development as Freedom*
Adam Smith's *The Wealth of Nations*
Nassim Nicholas Taleb's *The Black Swan: The Impact of the Highly Improbable*
Amos Tversky's & Daniel Kahneman's *Judgment under Uncertainty: Heuristics and Biases*
Mahbub Ul Haq's *Reflections on Human Development*
Max Weber's *The Protestant Ethic and the Spirit of Capitalism*

FEMINISM AND GENDER STUDIES

Judith Butler's *Gender Trouble*
Simone De Beauvoir's *The Second Sex*
Michel Foucault's *History of Sexuality*
Betty Friedan's *The Feminine Mystique*
Saba Mahmood's *The Politics of Piety: The Islamic Revival and the Feminist Subject*
Joan Wallach Scott's *Gender and the Politics of History*
Mary Wollstonecraft's *A Vindication of the Rights of Woman*
Virginia Woolf's *A Room of One's Own*

GEOGRAPHY

The Brundtland Report's *Our Common Future*
Rachel Carson's *Silent Spring*
Charles Darwin's *On the Origin of Species*
James Ferguson's *The Anti-Politics Machine*
Jane Jacobs's *The Death and Life of Great American Cities*
James Lovelock's *Gaia: A New Look at Life on Earth*
Amartya Sen's *Development as Freedom*
Mathis Wackernagel & William Rees's *Our Ecological Footprint*

HISTORY

Janet Abu-Lughod's *Before European Hegemony*
Benedict Anderson's *Imagined Communities*
Bernard Bailyn's *The Ideological Origins of the American Revolution*
Hanna Batatu's *The Old Social Classes And The Revolutionary Movements Of Iraq*
Christopher Browning's *Ordinary Men: Reserve Police Batallion 101 and the Final Solution in Poland*
Edmund Burke's *Reflections on the Revolution in France*
William Cronon's *Nature's Metropolis: Chicago And The Great West*
Alfred W. Crosby's *The Columbian Exchange*
Hamid Dabashi's *Iran: A People Interrupted*
David Brion Davis's *The Problem of Slavery in the Age of Revolution*
Nathalie Zemon Davis's *The Return of Martin Guerre*
Jared Diamond's *Guns, Germs & Steel: the Fate of Human Societies*
Frank Dikotter's *Mao's Great Famine*
John W Dower's *War Without Mercy: Race And Power In The Pacific War*
W. E. B. Du Bois's *The Souls of Black Folk*
Richard J. Evans's *In Defence of History*
Lucien Febvre's *The Problem of Unbelief in the 16th Century*
Sheila Fitzpatrick's *Everyday Stalinism*

Eric Foner's *Reconstruction: America's Unfinished Revolution, 1863-1877*
Michel Foucault's *Discipline and Punish*
Michel Foucault's *History of Sexuality*
Francis Fukuyama's *The End of History and the Last Man*
John Lewis Gaddis's *We Now Know: Rethinking Cold War History*
Ernest Gellner's *Nations and Nationalism*
Eugene Genovese's *Roll, Jordan, Roll: The World the Slaves Made*
Carlo Ginzburg's *The Night Battles*
Daniel Goldhagen's *Hitler's Willing Executioners*
Jack Goldstone's *Revolution and Rebellion in the Early Modern World*
Antonio Gramsci's *The Prison Notebooks*
Alexander Hamilton, John Jay & James Madison's *The Federalist Papers*
Christopher Hill's *The World Turned Upside Down*
Carole Hillenbrand's *The Crusades: Islamic Perspectives*
Thomas Hobbes's *Leviathan*
Eric Hobsbawm's *The Age Of Revolution*
John A. Hobson's *Imperialism: A Study*
Albert Hourani's *History of the Arab Peoples*
Samuel P. Huntington's *The Clash of Civilizations and the Remaking of World Order*
C. L. R. James's *The Black Jacobins*
Tony Judt's *Postwar: A History of Europe Since 1945*
Ernst Kantorowicz's *The King's Two Bodies: A Study in Medieval Political Theology*
Paul Kennedy's *The Rise and Fall of the Great Powers*
Ian Kershaw's *The "Hitler Myth": Image and Reality in the Third Reich*
John Maynard Keynes's *The General Theory of Employment, Interest and Money*
Charles P. Kindleberger's *Manias, Panics and Crashes*
Martin Luther King Jr's *Why We Can't Wait*
Henry Kissinger's *World Order: Reflections on the Character of Nations and the Course of History*
Thomas Kuhn's *The Structure of Scientific Revolutions*
Georges Lefebvre's *The Coming of the French Revolution*
John Locke's *Two Treatises of Government*
Niccolò Machiavelli's *The Prince*
Thomas Robert Malthus's *An Essay on the Principle of Population*
Mahmood Mamdani's *Citizen and Subject: Contemporary Africa And The Legacy Of Late Colonialism*
Karl Marx's *Capital*
Stanley Milgram's *Obedience to Authority*
John Stuart Mill's *On Liberty*
Thomas Paine's *Common Sense*
Thomas Paine's *Rights of Man*
Geoffrey Parker's *Global Crisis: War, Climate Change and Catastrophe in the Seventeenth Century*
Jonathan Riley-Smith's *The First Crusade and the Idea of Crusading*
Jean-Jacques Rousseau's *The Social Contract*
Joan Wallach Scott's *Gender and the Politics of History*
Theda Skocpol's *States and Social Revolutions*
Adam Smith's *The Wealth of Nations*
Timothy Snyder's *Bloodlands: Europe Between Hitler and Stalin*
Sun Tzu's *The Art of War*
Keith Thomas's *Religion and the Decline of Magic*
Thucydides's *The History of the Peloponnesian War*
Frederick Jackson Turner's *The Significance of the Frontier in American History*
Odd Arne Westad's *The Global Cold War: Third World Interventions And The Making Of Our Times*

The Macat Library By Discipline

Alexis De Tocqueville's *Democracy in America*
James Ferguson's *The Anti-Politics Machine*
Frank Dikotter's *Mao's Great Famine*
Sheila Fitzpatrick's *Everyday Stalinism*
Eric Foner's *Reconstruction: America's Unfinished Revolution, 1863-1877*
Milton Friedman's *Capitalism and Freedom*
Francis Fukuyama's *The End of History and the Last Man*
John Lewis Gaddis's *We Now Know: Rethinking Cold War History*
Ernest Gellner's *Nations and Nationalism*
David Graeber's *Debt: the First 5000 Years*
Antonio Gramsci's *The Prison Notebooks*
Alexander Hamilton, John Jay & James Madison's *The Federalist Papers*
Friedrich Hayek's *The Road to Serfdom*
Christopher Hill's *The World Turned Upside Down*
Thomas Hobbes's *Leviathan*
John A. Hobson's *Imperialism: A Study*
Samuel P. Huntington's *The Clash of Civilizations and the Remaking of World Order*
Tony Judt's *Postwar: A History of Europe Since 1945*
David C. Kang's *China Rising: Peace, Power and Order in East Asia*
Paul Kennedy's *The Rise and Fall of Great Powers*
Robert Keohane's *After Hegemony*
Martin Luther King Jr.'s *Why We Can't Wait*
Henry Kissinger's *World Order: Reflections on the Character of Nations and the Course of History*
John Locke's *Two Treatises of Government*
Niccolò Machiavelli's *The Prince*
Thomas Robert Malthus's *An Essay on the Principle of Population*
Mahmood Mamdani's *Citizen and Subject: Contemporary Africa And The Legacy Of
Late Colonialism*
Karl Marx's *Capital*
John Stuart Mill's *On Liberty*
John Stuart Mill's *Utilitarianism*
Hans Morgenthau's *Politics Among Nations*
Thomas Paine's *Common Sense*
Thomas Paine's *Rights of Man*
Thomas Piketty's *Capital in the Twenty-First Century*
Robert D. Putman's *Bowling Alone*
John Rawls's *Theory of Justice*
Jean-Jacques Rousseau's *The Social Contract*
Theda Skocpol's *States and Social Revolutions*
Adam Smith's *The Wealth of Nations*
Sun Tzu's *The Art of War*
Henry David Thoreau's *Civil Disobedience*
Thucydides's *The History of the Peloponnesian War*
Kenneth Waltz's *Theory of International Politics*
Max Weber's *Politics as a Vocation*
Odd Arne Westad's *The Global Cold War: Third World Interventions And The Making Of Our Times*

POSTCOLONIAL STUDIES

Roland Barthes's *Mythologies*
Frantz Fanon's *Black Skin, White Masks*
Homi K. Bhabha's *The Location of Culture*
Gustavo Gutiérrez's *A Theology of Liberation*
Edward Said's *Orientalism*
Gayatri Chakravorty Spivak's *Can the Subaltern Speak?*

The Macat Library By Discipline

PSYCHOLOGY

Gordon Allport's *The Nature of Prejudice*
Alan Baddeley & Graham Hitch's *Aggression: A Social Learning Analysis*
Albert Bandura's *Aggression: A Social Learning Analysis*
Leon Festinger's *A Theory of Cognitive Dissonance*
Sigmund Freud's *The Interpretation of Dreams*
Betty Friedan's *The Feminine Mystique*
Michael R. Gottfredson & Travis Hirschi's *A General Theory of Crime*
Eric Hoffer's *The True Believer: Thoughts on the Nature of Mass Movements*
William James's *Principles of Psychology*
Elizabeth Loftus's *Eyewitness Testimony*
A. H. Maslow's *A Theory of Human Motivation*
Stanley Milgram's *Obedience to Authority*
Steven Pinker's *The Better Angels of Our Nature*
Oliver Sacks's *The Man Who Mistook His Wife For a Hat*
Richard Thaler & Cass Sunstein's *Nudge: Improving Decisions About Health, Wealth and Happiness*
Amos Tversky's *Judgment under Uncertainty: Heuristics and Biases*
Philip Zimbardo's *The Lucifer Effect*

SCIENCE

Rachel Carson's *Silent Spring*
William Cronon's *Nature's Metropolis: Chicago And The Great West*
Alfred W. Crosby's *The Columbian Exchange*
Charles Darwin's *On the Origin of Species*
Richard Dawkin's *The Selfish Gene*
Thomas Kuhn's *The Structure of Scientific Revolutions*
Geoffrey Parker's *Global Crisis: War, Climate Change and Catastrophe in the Seventeenth Century*
Mathis Wackernagel & William Rees's *Our Ecological Footprint*

SOCIOLOGY

Michelle Alexander's *The New Jim Crow: Mass Incarceration in the Age of Colorblindness*
Gordon Allport's *The Nature of Prejudice*
Albert Bandura's *Aggression: A Social Learning Analysis*
Hanna Batatu's *The Old Social Classes And The Revolutionary Movements Of Iraq*
Ha-Joon Chang's *Kicking Away the Ladder*
W. E. B. Du Bois's *The Souls of Black Folk*
Émile Durkheim's *On Suicide*
Frantz Fanon's *Black Skin, White Masks*
Frantz Fanon's *The Wretched of the Earth*
Eric Foner's *Reconstruction: America's Unfinished Revolution, 1863-1877*
Eugene Genovese's *Roll, Jordan, Roll: The World the Slaves Made*
Jack Goldstone's *Revolution and Rebellion in the Early Modern World*
Antonio Gramsci's *The Prison Notebooks*
Richard Herrnstein & Charles A Murray's *The Bell Curve: Intelligence and Class Structure in American Life*
Eric Hoffer's *The True Believer: Thoughts on the Nature of Mass Movements*
Jane Jacobs's *The Death and Life of Great American Cities*
Robert Lucas's *Why Doesn't Capital Flow from Rich to Poor Countries?*
Jay Macleod's *Ain't No Makin' It: Aspirations and Attainment in a Low Income Neighborhood*
Elaine May's *Homeward Bound: American Families in the Cold War Era*
Douglas McGregor's *The Human Side of Enterprise*
C. Wright Mills's *The Sociological Imagination*

Thomas Piketty's *Capital in the Twenty-First Century*
Robert D. Putman's *Bowling Alone*
David Riesman's *The Lonely Crowd: A Study of the Changing American Character*
Edward Said's *Orientalism*
Joan Wallach Scott's *Gender and the Politics of History*
Theda Skocpol's *States and Social Revolutions*
Max Weber's *The Protestant Ethic and the Spirit of Capitalism*

THEOLOGY

Augustine's *Confessions*
Benedict's *Rule of St Benedict*
Gustavo Gutiérrez's *A Theology of Liberation*
Carole Hillenbrand's *The Crusades: Islamic Perspectives*
David Hume's *Dialogues Concerning Natural Religion*
Immanuel Kant's *Religion within the Boundaries of Mere Reason*
Ernst Kantorowicz's *The King's Two Bodies: A Study in Medieval Political Theology*
Søren Kierkegaard's *The Sickness Unto Death*
C. S. Lewis's *The Abolition of Man*
Saba Mahmood's *The Politics of Piety: The Islamic Revival and the Feminist Subject*
Baruch Spinoza's *Ethics*
Keith Thomas's *Religion and the Decline of Magic*

Macat Disciplines

Access the greatest ideas and thinkers across entire disciplines, including

INEQUALITY

Ha-Joon Chang's, *Kicking Away the Ladder*

David Graeber's, *Debt: The First 5000 Years*

Robert E. Lucas's, *Why Doesn't Capital Flow from Rich To Poor Countries?*

Thomas Piketty's, *Capital in the Twenty-First Century*

Amartya Sen's, *Inequality Re-Examined*

Mahbub Ul Haq's, *Reflections on Human Development*

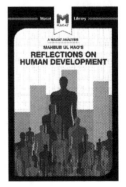

Macat analyses are available from all good bookshops and libraries.

Access hundreds of analyses through one, multimedia tool.
Join free for one month **library.macat.com**

Macat Disciplines

Access the greatest ideas and thinkers across entire disciplines, including

CRIMINOLOGY

Michelle Alexander's
*The New Jim Crow:
Mass Incarceration in the
Age of Colorblindness*

**Michael R. Gottfredson
& Travis Hirschi's**
A General Theory of Crime

Elizabeth Loftus's
Eyewitness Testimony

**Richard Herrnstein
& Charles A. Murray's**
*The Bell Curve: Intelligence and
Class Structure in American Life*

Jay Macleod's
*Ain't No Makin' It:
Aspirations and Attainment in a
Low-Income Neighborhood*

Philip Zimbardo's
The Lucifer Effect

Macat Disciplines

Access the greatest ideas and thinkers across entire disciplines, including

POSTCOLONIAL STUDIES

Roland Barthes's *Mythologies*
Frantz Fanon's *Black Skin, White Masks*
Homi K. Bhabha's *The Location of Culture*
Gustavo Gutiérrez's *A Theology of Liberation*
Edward Said's *Orientalism*
Gayatri Chakravorty Spivak's *Can the Subaltern Speak?*

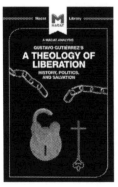
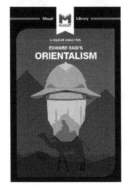

Macat analyses are available from all good bookshops and libraries.

Access hundreds of analyses through one, multimedia tool.
Join free for one month **library.macat.com**

Macat Disciplines

Access the greatest ideas and thinkers across entire disciplines, including

GLOBALIZATION

Arjun Appadurai's, *Modernity at Large: Cultural Dimensions of Globalisation*

James Ferguson's, *The Anti-Politics Machine*

Geert Hofstede's, *Culture's Consequences*

Amartya Sen's, *Development as Freedom*

Macat Pairs

Analyse historical and modern issues from opposite sides of an argument. Pairs include:

HOW TO RUN AN ECONOMY

John Maynard Keynes's
The General Theory OF Employment, Interest and Money

Classical economics suggests that market economies are self-correcting in times of recession or depression, and tend toward full employment and output. But English economist John Maynard Keynes disagrees.

In his ground-breaking 1936 study *The General Theory*, Keynes argues that traditional economics has misunderstood the causes of unemployment. Employment is not determined by the price of labor; it is directly linked to demand. Keynes believes market economies are by nature unstable, and so require government intervention. Spurred on by the social catastrophe of the Great Depression of the 1930s, he sets out to revolutionize the way the world thinks

Milton Friedman's
The Role of Monetary Policy

Friedman's 1968 paper changed the course of economic theory. In just 17 pages, he demolished existing theory and outlined an effective alternate monetary policy designed to secure 'high employment, stable prices and rapid growth.'

Friedman demonstrated that monetary policy plays a vital role in broader economic stability and argued that economists got their monetary policy wrong in the 1950s and 1960s by misunderstanding the relationship between inflation and unemployment. Previous generations of economists had believed that governments could permanently decrease unemployment by permitting inflation—and vice versa. Friedman's most original contribution was to show that this supposed trade-off is an illusion that only works in the short term.

Macat analyses are available from all good bookshops and libraries.

Access hundreds of analyses through one, multimedia tool.
Join free for one month **library.macat.com**

Macat Disciplines

Access the greatest ideas and thinkers across entire disciplines, including

TOTALITARIANISM

Sheila Fitzpatrick's, *Everyday Stalinism*
Ian Kershaw's, *The "Hitler Myth"*
Timothy Snyder's, *Bloodlands*

Macat Pairs

Analyse historical and modern issues from opposite sides of an argument. Pairs include:

INTERNATIONAL RELATIONS IN THE 21ST CENTURY

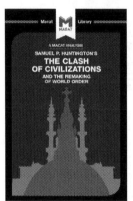

Samuel P. Huntington's
The Clash of Civilisations

In his highly influential 1996 book, Huntington offers a vision of a post-Cold War world in which conflict takes place not between competing ideologies but between cultures. The worst clash, he argues, will be between the Islamic world and the West: the West's arrogance and belief that its culture is a "gift" to the world will come into conflict with Islam's obstinacy and concern that its culture is under attack from a morally decadent "other."

Clash inspired much debate between different political schools of thought. But its greatest impact came in helping define American foreign policy in the wake of the 2001 terrorist attacks in New York and Washington.

Francis Fukuyama's
The End of History and the Last Man

Published in 1992, *The End of History and the Last Man* argues that capitalist democracy is the final destination for all societies. Fukuyama believed democracy triumphed during the Cold War because it lacks the "fundamental contradictions" inherent in communism and satisfies our yearning for freedom and equality. Democracy therefore marks the endpoint in the evolution of ideology, and so the "end of history." There will still be "events," but no fundamental change in ideology.

Macat analyses are available from all good bookshops and libraries.

Access hundreds of analyses through one, multimedia tool.
Join free for one month **library.macat.com**

Macat Pairs

Analyse historical and modern issues from opposite sides of an argument. Pairs include:

ARE WE FUNDAMENTALLY GOOD - OR BAD?

Steven Pinker's
The Better Angels of Our Nature

Stephen Pinker's gloriously optimistic 2011 book argues that, despite humanity's biological tendency toward violence, we are, in fact, less violent today than ever before. To prove his case, Pinker lays out pages of detailed statistical evidence. For him, much of the credit for the decline goes to the eighteenth-century Enlightenment movement, whose ideas of liberty, tolerance, and respect for the value of human life filtered down through society and affected how people thought. That psychological change led to behavioral change—and overall we became more peaceful. Critics countered that humanity could never overcome the biological urge toward violence; others argued that Pinker's statistics were flawed.

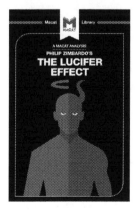

Philip Zimbardo's
The Lucifer Effect

Some psychologists believe those who commit cruelty are innately evil. Zimbardo disagrees. In *The Lucifer Effect*, he argues that sometimes good people do evil things simply because of the situations they find themselves in, citing many historical examples to illustrate his point. Zimbardo details his 1971 Stanford prison experiment, where ordinary volunteers playing guards in a mock prison rapidly became abusive. But he also describes the tortures committed by US army personnel in Iraq's Abu Ghraib prison in 2003—and how he himself testified in defence of one of those guards. committed by US army personnel in Iraq's Abu Ghraib prison in 2003—and how he himself testified in defence of one of those guards.

Macat analyses are available from all good bookshops and libraries.

Access hundreds of analyses through one, multimedia tool.
Join free for one month **library.macat.com**

Macat Pairs

*Analyse historical and modern issues from opposite sides of an argument.
Pairs include:*

HOW WE RELATE TO EACH OTHER AND SOCIETY

Jean-Jacques Rousseau's
The Social Contract

Rousseau's famous work sets out the radical concept of the 'social contract': a give-and-take relationship between individual freedom and social order.

If people are free to do as they like, governed only by their own sense of justice, they are also vulnerable to chaos and violence. To avoid this, Rousseau proposes, they should agree to give up some freedom to benefit from the protection of social and political organization. But this deal is only just if societies are led by the collective needs and desires of the people, and able to control the private interests of individuals. For Rousseau, the only legitimate form of government is rule by the people.

Robert D. Putnam's
Bowling Alone

In *Bowling Alone*, Robert Putnam argues that Americans have become disconnected from one another and from the institutions of their common life, and investigates the consequences of this change.

Looking at a range of indicators, from membership in formal organizations to the number of invitations being extended to informal dinner parties, Putnam demonstrates that Americans are interacting less and creating less "social capital" – with potentially disastrous implications for their society.

It would be difficult to overstate the impact of *Bowling Alone*, one of the most frequently cited social science publications of the last half-century.

Macat analyses are available from all good bookshops and libraries.

Access hundreds of analyses through one, multimedia tool.
Join free for one month **library.macat.com**